W9-BPK-702

INTRODUCING ISSUES WITH

OPPOSING VIEWPOINTS®

THE DEATH PENALTY

INTRODUCING
ISSUES
WITH

OPPOSING VIEWPOINTS®

THE DEATH PENALTY

Other books in the Introducing Issues
with Opposing Viewpoints series:

INTRODUCING
ISSUES
WITH

OPPOSING VIEWPOINTS®

THE DEATH PENALTY

Lauri S. Friedman, *Book Editor*

Bruce Glassman, *Vice President*
Bonnie Szumski, *Publisher, Series Editor*
Helen Cothran, *Managing Editor*

OPPOSING
VIEWPOINTS®
SERIES

GREENHAVEN PRESS
An imprint of Thomson Gale, a part of The Thomson Corporation

THOMSON
™
GALE

Detroit • New York • San Francisco • San Diego • New Haven, Conn. • Waterville, Maine • London • Munich

THOMSON

™

GALE

LIBRARY OF CONGRESS CATALOGING-IN-PUBLICATION DATA

The death penalty / Lauri S. Friedman, book editor.
    p. cm. — (Introducing issues with opposing viewpoints)
  Includes bibliographical references and index.
  ISBN 0-7377-3341-1 (lib. bdg. : alk. paper)
   1. Capital punishment—United States. 2. Capital punishment. I. Friedman, Lauri S. II. Series.
   HV8699.U5D35 2006
   364.66'0973—dc22
                                                          2005040401

Printed in the United States of America

CONTENTS

Indulging in a wide spectrum of ideas, beliefs, and perspectives is a critical cornerstone of democracy. After all, it is often debates over differences of opinion, such as whether to legalize abortion, how to treat prisoners, or when to enact the death penalty that shape our society and drive it forward. Such diversity of thought is frequently regarded as the hallmark of a healthy and civilized culture. As the Reverend Clifford Schutjer of the First Congregational Church in Mansfield, Ohio, declared in a 2001 sermon, "Surrounding oneself with only like-minded people, restricting what we listen to or read only to what we find agreeable is irresponsible. Refusing to entertain doubts once we make up our minds is a subtle but deadly form of arrogance." With this advice in mind, Introducing Issues with Opposing Viewpoints books aim to open readers' minds to the critically divergent views that comprise our world's most important debates.

Introducing Issues with Opposing Viewpoints simplifies for students the enormous and often overwhelming mass of material now available via print and electronic media. Collected in every volume is an array of opinions that captures the essence of a particular controversy or topic. Introducing Issues with Opposing Viewpoints books embody the spirit of nineteenth-century journalist Charles A. Dana's axiom: "Fight for your opinions, but do not believe that they contain the whole truth, or the only truth." Absorbing such contrasting opinions teaches students to analyze the strength of an argument and compare it to its opposition. From this process readers can inform and strengthen their own opinions, or be exposed to new information that will change their minds. Introducing Issues with Opposing Viewpoints is a mosaic of different voices. The authors are statesmen, pundits, academics, journalists, corporations, and ordinary people who have felt compelled to share their experiences and ideas in a public forum. Their words have been collected from newspapers, journals, books, speeches, interviews, and the Internet, the fastest growing body of opinionated material in the world.

Introducing Issues with Opposing Viewpoints shares many of the well-known features of its critically acclaimed parent series, Opposing Viewpoints. The articles are presented in a pro/con format, allowing readers to absorb divergent perspectives side by side. Active reading questions preface each viewpoint, requiring the student to approach the material thoughtfully and carefully. Useful charts, graphs, and cartoons supplement each article. A thorough introduction provides readers with crucial background on an issue. An annotated bibliography points the reader toward articles, books, and Web sites that contain additional information on the topic. An appendix of organizations to contact contains a wide variety of charities, nonprofit organizations, political groups, and private enterprises that each hold a position on the issue at hand. Finally, a comprehensive index allows readers to locate content quickly and efficiently.

Introducing Issues with Opposing Viewpoints is also significantly different from Opposing Viewpoints. As the series title implies, its presentation will help introduce students to the concept of opposing viewpoints, and learn to use this material to aid in critical writing and debate. The series' four-color, accessible format makes the books attractive and inviting to readers of all levels. In addition, each viewpoint has been carefully edited to maximize a reader's understanding of the content. Short but thorough viewpoints capture the essence of an argument. A substantial, thought-provoking essay question placed at the end of each viewpoint asks the student to further investigate the issues raised in the viewpoint, compare and contrast two authors' arguments, or consider how one might go about forming an opinion on the topic at hand. Each viewpoint contains sidebars that include at-a-glance information and handy statistics. A Facts About section located in the back of the book further supplies students with relevant facts and figures.

Following in the tradition of the Opposing Viewpoints series, Greenhaven Press continues to provide readers with invaluable exposure to the controversial issues that shape our world. As John Stuart Mill once wrote: "The only way in which a human being can make some approach to knowing the whole of a subject is by hearing what can be said about it by persons of every variety of opinion and studying all modes in which it can be looked at by every character of mind. No wise man ever acquired his wisdom in any mode but this." It is to this principle that Introducing Issues with Opposing Viewpoints books are dedicated.

INTRODUCTION

"[The death penalty] puts the U.S. in an embarrassing international position on human rights."

—Victor Streib, Ohio Northern University Law School

"The right to freedom and to life are both fundamental human rights. [But] both such rights may be forfeited when criminals commit specific acts, such as the rape/torture/murder of children."

—Dudley Sharp, director of Justice for All

The United States' use of the death penalty is an increasingly controversial topic, both at home and abroad. Each year, more and more countries either abolish the death penalty as an acceptable form of punishment, or put such severe limitations on it that it is essentially rendered obsolete. Interestingly, on issues such as the death penalty, America ranks with some of its most avowed enemies, such as Iran, and against many of its staunch allies, such as Europe and many countries in the Americas. Critics of capital punishment argue that the U.S. support of the death penalty uncomfortably places it in the company of some of the worst human rights violators in the world. On the other hand, proponents of the death penalty argue that America's use of the practice is fair, thorough, and just, and does not constitute a violation of human rights. This debate over whether the death penalty constitutes a violation of human rights is central to the issue of capital punishment in the United States and around the world.

Human rights activists denounce the death penalty as a violation of human rights. As a practitioner of capital punishment, the United States finds itself in the company of such nations as Nigeria, Pakistan, Saudi Arabia, Congo, and Yemen, all of which are regularly assailed by the international community and the United States for committing other kinds of human rights violations, such as exploiting child labor or discriminating against women. Critics of the death penalty argue that the

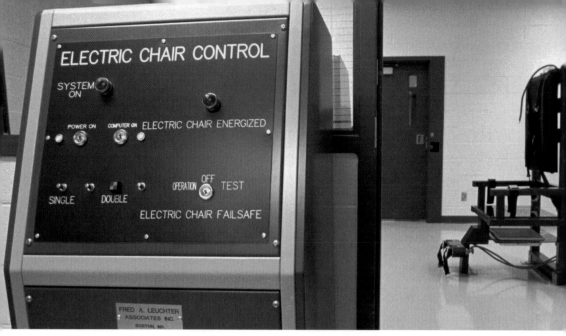

The electric chair is one of five legal means of execution in the United States. The other methods are hanging, firing squad, lethal injection, and death by lethal gas.

United States cannot hope to eradicate some human rights violations around the world when it is seen by many nations as a human rights violator itself. Given its frequent use of the death penalty, and particularly its controversial execution of mentally disabled people, Amnesty International has declared, "In the eyes of many members of the international community of nations, any further attempt by the U.S. government to boast about its deep commitment to human rights protection will undoubtedly be seen as little more than arrogant hypocrisy."

These critics charge that America's commitment to the death penalty has significantly cost it in international reputation and influence. In 2001, the United States was voted off the International Commission on Human Rights for the first time in that panel's fifty-four-year history. While there were many factors in that decision, America's use of the death penalty was one charge embraced by those nations that argued against America's inclusion on the commission. Similarly, in 2003, another commission, the Inter-American Commission on Human Rights, eliminated the U.S. seat based in part on its observance of the death penalty. In yet another alienating move, in 2001 the Council of Europe, a political organization representing forty-five European nations, passed a resolution that demanded the United States establish a moratorium on executions or face a revocation of their status within the council. Many critics charge these events have weakened America's position as an influential world leader. As Professor Connie De La Vega says, "If the United States wants to regain its role as promoter and protector of human rights around the world, it first needs to address its own violations of internationally recognized standards."

On the other side of the issue, however, proponents of the death penalty contend that capital punishment in the United States is used selectively and with great accuracy. Indeed, they argue that the

Opponents of the death penalty protest outside a Florida prison during a 2002 execution.

painstaking efforts that go into verifying an inmate's guilt prior to execution is proof that the United States deeply respects human rights and does not carelessly or callously execute. As Diane Clements of Justice for All, a pro–death penalty organization, points out, "If 40 murderers are executed in a year when there were 15,000 murders, that's not a disproportionate use of capital punishment. Where's the human rights problem?"

Furthermore, proponents argue that the United States overwhelmingly uses lethal injection to execute murderers, which is considered to be the most humane form of execution there is. On these grounds they reject comparisons with Saudi Arabia, a nation that engages in public executions, and goes so far as to chop off body parts as punishment for crime. Throughout its history the United States has also been dedicat-

Proponents of the death penalty show their support for the execution of Oklahoma City bomber Timothy McVeigh. They believe McVeigh deserved to die for the many lives he took.

ed to improving and preserving children's rights, women's rights, workers' rights, and democracy both at home and abroad. As Gare Smith of the U.S. State Department says, "The U.S. isn't perfect. But you would be hard pressed to come up with a country that has a better human rights record than we do."

Finally, those who reject the suggestion that the death penalty constitutes a violation of human rights argue that those on death row have already committed the gravest crime against humanity: They took an innocent life, and caused inexpressible grief to forever shadow a victim's family, friends, and loved ones. From this perspective, the death penalty is seen by many to be an act of justice that upholds the sanctity of life. As death penalty advocate Wesley Lowe puts it, "The death penalty is a punishment for a human rights violation, not a human rights violation itself. Anyone with any amount of moral judgment and coherence would recognize and respect that difference."

Clearly, the death penalty remains one of America's most vigorously debated issues, both internationally and domestically. The viewpoints presented in *Introducing Issues with Opposing Viewpoints: The Death Penalty* offer further insight into the key debates surrounding this controversial topic.

CHAPTER 1

Is the Death Penalty Just?

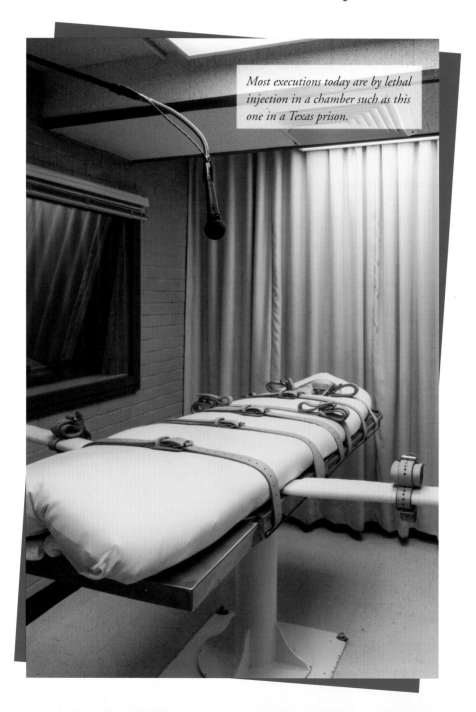

Most executions today are by lethal injection in a chamber such as this one in a Texas prison.

The Death Penalty Is Just

Dudley Sharp

> *"The punishment of murderers has been earned by the pain and suffering they have imposed on their victims."*

In the following viewpoint, Dudley Sharp argues that executing murderers is the only way to justly punish them for their crimes. The author recognizes that extinguishing a murderer's life can never bring back a lost loved one, but argues it is the best way for families of victims to obtain closure and justice. Despite claims that the death penalty is fraught with error and that innocent people may be executed, Sharp contends that it is a nearly foolproof process that doles out justice well. He concludes by arguing that those who take life do not deserve to keep their own, and so the death penalty dispenses the greatest measure of justice that can be achieved short of restoring life to someone who has been killed.

Dudley Sharp is the vice president of Justice for All, a not-for-profit criminal justice reform organization that supports the death penalty. Sharp has written extensively on this issue; his articles have appeared in the *Wall Street Journal* and *World & I*, from which this viewpoint was taken.

There is nothing quite like hanging out with your best friend. Jenny Ertman, 14, and Elizabeth Peña, 16, shared their hopes and dreams with each other. Like millions of other teenagers, they liked to have fun, to laugh and smile. One summer evening in Houston, Texas, they shared their last moments on earth together—their own murders.

They were late returning home and took a shortcut through the woods, next to some railroad tracks. They ran into a gang initiation. They were both raped: orally, anally, and vaginally. The gang members laughed about the virgin blood they spilled. When they had finished, they beat and strangled the girls. But Jenny and Elizabeth wouldn't die. With all their strength, with their souls still holding on to the beautiful lives before them, they fought for life.

The gang worked harder. The girls were strangled with belts and shoelaces, stomped on and beaten. Their dreams disappeared as life seeped away from their broken bodies.

Their parents are left to visit empty rooms, to cry upon the beds of their daughters and think what could have been. How beautiful Elizabeth would have been in her prom dress. Her corsage was replaced by the flowers on her grave.

And Jenny's future children, would their grandparents have spoiled them? You know the answer. The immutable joy of grandchildren's laughter was silenced by the cruel selfishness of murder.

The Most Appropriate Punishment

Sometimes, the death penalty is simply the most appropriate punishment for the vile crime committed. In such cases, jurors are given the choice between a death sentence and a variety of life sentences, depending upon the jurisdiction. It is never easy for juries to give a death sentence. Neither hatred nor revenge is part of their deliberations. The search for justice determines the punishment.

The murder of the innocent is undeserved. The punishment of murderers has been earned by the pain and suffering they have imposed on their victims. Execution cannot truly represent justice, because there is no recompense to balance the weight of murder. For some crimes, it represents the only just punishment available on earth.

Today, much more than justice is part of the death penalty discussion. Opponents are relentlessly attacking the penalty process itself. They insist that it is so fraught with error and caprice that it should be abandoned. At the very least, they say, America should impose a national moratorium so the system can be reviewed.

The families of twin murder victims pose at a memorial erected at the crime site. Some families of murder victims view the death penalty as just punishment.

The Death Penalty Is Reliable

The leading salvo in those claims is that 101 innocent people have been released from death row with evidence of their innocence. The number is a fraud. Unfortunately, both the international media and, most predictably, the U.S. media have swallowed such claims and passed them along to the public. . . .

The source for these claims is the Death Penalty Information Center (DPIC), the leading source of antideath penalty material in the United States. Richard Dieter, head of the DPIC, has admitted, in the June 6, 2000, *ABA Journal,* that his group makes no distinction between the legally innocent ("I got off death row because of legal error") and the actually innocent ("I had no connection to the murder") cases. Although the DPIC has attempted to revise its standards for establishing innocence, none of the various contortions even suggests actual innocence.

As everyone knows, the debate is about the actually innocent. To strengthen their case, death penalty opponents have broadened their "innocent" count by cases that don't merit that description. On June 20

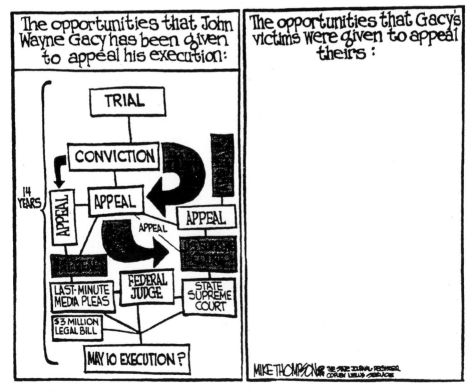

Source: Thompson. © 1994 by Copley News Service. Reproduced by permission.

[2002], for example, the Florida Commission on Capital Cases released its review of 23 death sentence cases that the DPIC had called into question. Its conclusion was that in only 4 of those cases were there doubts as to guilt.

Though the DPIC claims that 101 cases were released from death row with evidence of innocence, the actual number is closer to 30. That is 30 cases out of 7,000 sentenced to death since 1973. It appears that the death penalty may well be this country's most accurate criminal sanction, when taking into account the percentage of actual innocent convicted (0.4 percent) and the thoroughness of preventing those allegedly innocent from being executed (100 percent).

Of all the world's social and governmental institutions that put innocents at risk, I can find only one, the U.S. death penalty, that has no proof of an innocent killed since 1900. Can you think of another? . . .

The Death Penalty Honors Life

This brings me back to where I started: justice. Some say that executions show a contempt for human life, but the opposite is true. We would hope that a brutal rape may result in a life sentence. Why? We value freedom so highly that we take freedom away as punishment. If freedom were not valued, taking it away would be no sanction.

Life is considered even more precious. Therefore, the death penalty is considered the severest sanction for the most horrible of crimes. Even murderers tell us that they value life (their own) more than freedom. That is why over 99 percent of convicted capital murderers seek a life sentence, not a death sentence, during the punishment phase of their trials.

Even some of those traditionally against capital punishment have decided that some crimes are justly punished with death. [Oklahoma City bomber] Timothy McVeigh's 2001 execution was thought a just punishment by 81 percent of the American people, reflecting an all-time high of support. When 168 innocents were murdered [on April 19, 1995, in the terrorist attack in Oklahoma City] including 19 children whom

Timothy McVeigh (inset) killed 168 people when he bombed the Oklahoma City Federal Building (above) in 1995.

McVeigh described as "collateral damage," the collective conscience of the American people reached an overwhelming consensus. A Gallup poll, released on May 20 [2002], shows that 72 percent supported the death penalty, with nearly half those polled saying the sanction is not imposed enough.

The Goodness in People Stands Out

Why didn't I invoke the murder of 3,100 innocents on September 11 [2001]? Because the murder of one Jenny Ertman is enough—much too much. Which one of the murdered innocents was more valuable than another? Was one child blown apart in Oklahoma City not enough? Was a father forever lost on September 11 not enough? A son? A granddaughter?

Is it the numbers, at all? No, it is the realization that those innocent lives, so willfully ripped from us, represent individuals who contributed to someone's life and happiness. The sheer numbers of murders committed each year may numb us beyond what an individual murder can. But that is only because we must shield ourselves from the absolute horror represented by one innocent murdered. It is a matter of emotional self-preservation.

This woman wears a T-shirt advocating the death penalty for Timothy McVeigh. Eighty-one percent of Americans polled believed that he should die.

Often, in the most horrible of times, we find that the goodness in people stands out. At one point during the attack, Jenny was able to escape and run away. Elizabeth's cries brought Jenny back in a fruitless attempt to aid her friend. Love, friendship, and devotion overcame fear.

Of the six attackers who brutalized these girls for over an hour, five received the death penalty. The sixth was too young to prosecute for death. And why did five separate juries give death? Justice.

EVALUATING THE AUTHORS' ARGUMENTS:

In the viewpoint you just read, the author argues that the death penalty honors life. In the following viewpoint, the author argues that the death penalty only leads to more death. After reading both viewpoints, which view do you find more convincing? Why?

The Death Penalty Is Unjust

Susannah Sheffer

"Pain isn't something you can get rid of by transferring it to someone else."

In the following viewpoint, Susannah Sheffer profiles the family members of murder victims to show that the death penalty is an unjust form of punishment that does not help the people who grieve for their victim. Several people who have experienced the murder of a family member express their opposition to the death penalty, saying that it would only create more death and suffering while doing nothing to ease their own pain. One man, who lost his daughter in the Oklahoma City bombing of April 1995, realizes that the death penalty is more about revenge and hatred than it is about justice. The author concludes by saying that the death penalty is a misplaced attempt to offer grieving people peace, which can only come from speaking about one's pain and having others understand and acknowledge it.

Susannah Sheffer has written for Murder Victims' Families for Reconciliation, a group that opposes the death penalty and works to change the criminal justice system. She is the author of four books, including *A Life Worth Living: Selected Letters of John Holt* and *A Sense of Self: Listening to Home Schooled Adolescent Girls.*

AS YOU READ, CONSIDER THE FOLLOWING QUESTIONS:
1. Why did Renny Cushing oppose sentencing his father's murderer to death?
2. What year was the death penalty reinstated in the United States?
3. According to the author, what makes execution seem like an attractive punishment?

It's a striking sight: about 40 people crowded on to a small stage, looking out at the audience. One after the other they speak, saying their names and then the name of the member of their family who was murdered. We hear of mothers, fathers, sons, daughters, sisters, brothers, grandparents. Each statement contains an entire horror, a story the speakers are not telling now but the impact of which is palpable behind their words. Each speaker adds after this, 'And I oppose the death penalty.'

The members of Murder Victims' Families for Reconciliation[1] are unusual in the United States. In a country that has executed 682 people since the death penalty was reinstated in 1976 and has about 3,800 sitting on death row today, most people assume murder victims' families are crying out for executions. Prosecutors seeking the death penalty righteously claim to be seeking justice for the grieving families and giving them what they want and need. If you happen to be opposing the death penalty on some other grounds—its racism, its cost, its failure to deter—inevitably the person taking the other side of the argument will offer what they believe is the ultimate challenge: 'But what if someone in *your* family were murdered? How would you feel then?'

Victims Against the Death Penalty

When Renny Cushing talks about how he felt after his father was murdered, he uses phrases like 'emotionally filleted'. He talks about the searing shock, the emptiness, the incomprehension. The idea that his father would open the door of his home one ordinary June evening and be greeted by a shotgun blast which would rip his chest apart in front of his wife of 37 years—how could Renny possibly have imagined this. How could he have imagined touching the blood on his father's face as

---

1. Murder Victims' Families for Reconciliation is a group that opposes the death penalty and works to change the criminal justice system.

he lay on the hospital gurney. Or going to the telephone and trying to find words to tell his brothers and sisters that their father had just been murdered for no reason they could fathom. . . .

The pain of that night is a pain that will mark the surviving Cushings for ever. When you talk to Renny now, 12 years after the murder, you can see that in some way he is still trying to figure out how to bear it. But one thing he has known from the beginning is that pain isn't something you can get rid of by transferring it to someone else. 'Sometimes people think it's a zero-sum game,' he says. 'They think if they can make someone else feel pain, theirs will go away. I just don't think it works that way.'

Renny Cushing (right) talks to the press outside a Connecticut prison as an inmate is executed in 2005. Despite the fact his father was murdered, Cushing opposes the death penalty.

Renny's interest in reducing violence, rather than adding to it, not only means that he opposes the death penalty. It also means that when he ran into the son of his father's murderer outside the courthouse one day, he understood that nothing would be gained by having that son lose a father too. 'I knew that to kill somebody else not only wouldn't honour my father's life; it would create another grieving family.'

The Death Penalty Is About Revenge and Hate

It took some time, but Bud Welch was able to come to the same realisation. Bud's daughter Julie Marie was killed in the bombing of the Oklahoma City Federal Building in April 1995. When Bud travels the country and tells about the day, audiences are drawn into one particular heart of a tragedy that they felt vividly, and in some sense collectively, when it originally took place. Bud talks about how wrecked he felt after the bombing, how strong was his desire to retaliate by killing Timothy McVeigh and Terry Nichols—the convicted bombers—himself. When he learned that President Bill Clinton and Attorney General Janet Reno would seek the death penalty, he looked forward to it, 'because here I had been crushed, I had been hurt, and that was the big fix.'

What do you do with the hurting? For weeks Bud smoked too much, drank too much, felt what he now recalls as a kind of temporary insanity. Then, about nine months after the bombing, he went down to the place where it happened and stood under an old American elm that had survived that April day. He let his mind wander to the upcoming trials and the likely executions,[2] and he said to himself, 'How's that going to help me? It isn't going to bring Julie back.' He realised that the death penalty 'is all about revenge and hate, and revenge and hate is why Julie and 167 others are dead today.' Gradually, Bud realised that he didn't want the killers executed. Before long, he was making his viewpoint publicly known. . . .

"The Highest Agony"

It's hard to find a word for this. It's something like reconciliation, though not necessarily in the sense of forgiving and certainly not with any element of forgetting. It is something like saying, a terrible thing happened

2. McVeigh was executed on June 11, 2001.

and I cannot go back so I have to find a way to keep walking, wounds and all.

The more time one spends with families of murder victims, the deeper is one's sense that what is wanted, maybe even more than revenge, is recognition and acknowledgement of the harm done. Vengeance says *that'll show him,* and it may be the desire to show that is really most

Mourners pray during a candlelight vigil to mark the ten-year anniversary of the Oklahoma City bombing. Taking part in such vigils can help some survivors cope with their grief.

Source: Stantis. © 2001 by Copley News Service. Reproduced by permission.

primary—the desire to speak the truth of one's pain and have it met with acknowledgement.

Paula Kurland, whose daughter Mitzi was raped and murdered by Jonathan Nobles, participated in Texas's Victim-Offender Reconciliation programme, where she was given the opportunity to meet with Nobles while he awaited execution on death row. She approached the meeting carrying a photograph of her daughter, and explained to the television reporter who was following the event, 'Jonathan is going to see what he took.'

They sat across from each other for two hours, separated by glass, and what Jonathan was forced to do in those hours was see—see what he took, see what he had done. . . . 'The sight of his own crimes is the highest agony a man can know,' wrote [playwright] Arthur Miller. Maybe it is. Yet unlike the pain of further violence, this agony of acknowledgement and recognition seems somehow redemptive, or at least part way towards healing. . . .

Some Wounds Cannot Close

Execution is attractive because it seems to match the original horror, to exact measure for measure. It seems a way of doing something. It must have been this impulse that led a friend of the Cushing family to say to Renny, as he passed him in the supermarket soon after his father's murderers had been apprehended, 'I hope they fry those people so your family can have some peace.'

Yet peace and comfort may actually consist of something quite different. The hardest thing for a society to accept may be that some wounds cannot close, not all the way. What we need to learn how to do may be in some ways more difficult than offering retribution. . . .

Maybe we need to learn to keep company with the pain that murder causes. Not minimising it, not trying to displace it, but aligning ourselves with it so that in time some truly helpful responses might become apparent, or some ideas about preventing it from happening again, so that when survivors stand before us and speak of their loss, we are able to meet their gaze, feel its impact and not look away.

EVALUATING THE AUTHORS' ARGUMENTS:

In this viewpoint and the one before it, both authors agree that the families of murder victims suffer immeasurable pain when a loved one is murdered. However, each author comes to a very different conclusion about the justice offered by the death penalty. In your opinion, is justice served by executing a murderer? Why or why not? Explain your answer.

The Death Penalty Is Cruel and Unusual Punishment

Vittorio Bufacchi and Laura Fairrie

"'No matter how "humane" an execution we devise, it is still a violation of human dignity.'"

In the following viewpoint, Vittorio Bufacchi and Laura Fairrie argue that execution by any method constitutes cruel and unusual punishment. Electrocution, the preferred method of execution in the United States until the late 1990s, has caused prisoners to experience horrific deaths that involve burning flesh and pervasive bleeding. Although most states now use lethal injection to execute prisoners, the authors argue this method continues to violate civilized society's commitment to avoiding cruel and unusual punishments. Although it appears more peaceful than electrocution, in reality lethal injection subjects the prisoner to a torturous death that is too often botched or the product of prolonged suffering. The authors conclude that it is impossible to ever devise a form of execution that is truly humane and thus capital punishment will always amount to a legitimized form of torture.

Vittorio Bufacchi teaches philosophy at University College in Cork, Ireland. Laura Fairrie produces and directs documentaries on current affairs.

AS YOU READ, CONSIDER THE FOLLOWING QUESTIONS:
1. What does warden Don Cabana mean when he says that lethal injection merely "sanitizes" the process of capital punishment?
2. How many states continue to use electrocution as a method of execution?
3. During a lethal injection, three substances are injected into a prisoner. According to the authors, what is the purpose of the first and second substances?

The idea that capital punishment is not torture is based on the historical assumption that there are humane ways of executing people. The search for ever more humane methods of execution began at least as early as the eighteenth century and the birth of the guillotine. The guillotine was proposed as more humane than existing methods of execution because it was supposed to terminate life more swiftly and efficiently. Dr. Guillotin, the inventor of this new death machine, explained to the National Constituent Assembly of France in 1789, "The criminal shall be decapitated and this will be done solely by means of a simple machine: it falls like thunder; the head flies off; blood spurts; and the man is no more!"

The tension between an abhorrence of torture and an enthusiasm for the death penalty has been most acute in the United States. It has led to repeated, and in our opinion, fruitless, efforts to follow the path set by Dr. Guillotin: using science and technology to find a humane, that is, quick and painless, way to kill prisoners. These efforts have taken the U.S. from hanging to electrocution to lethal gas to lethal injection. . . .

A Long Line of Horrific Executions

Death by electrocution is still plagued by botched executions involving unanticipated problems and prolonged agony for those condemned. Here is one eyewitness account of Alabama's electrocution of John Louis Evans on April 12, 1983:

> At 8:30 P.M. the first jolt of 1900 volts of electricity passed through Mr. Evans' body. It lasted thirty seconds. Sparks and flames erupted from the electrode tied to Mr. Evans' left leg. His body slammed

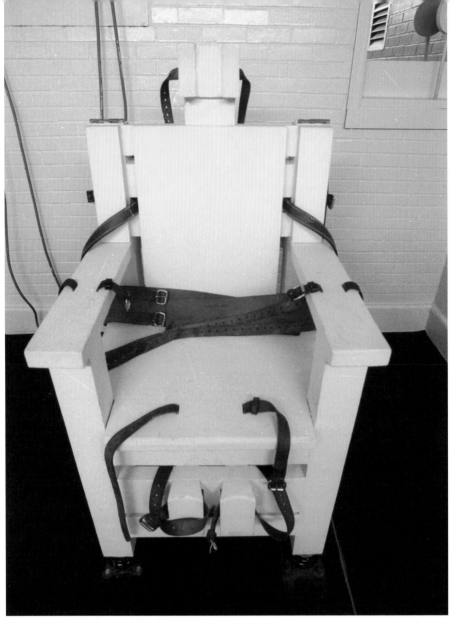

Execution by the electric chair was once thought to be a humane method of execution, but witnesses have testified that it is a gruesome, painful death.

against the straps holding him in the electric chair and his fist clenched permanently. The electrode apparently burst from the strap holding it in place. A large puff of grayish smoke and sparks poured out from under the hood that covered Mr. Evans' face. An overpowering stench of burnt flesh and clothing began pervading the witness room. Two doctors examined Mr. Evans and declared that he was not dead. The electrode on the left leg was refastened. At 8:34 P.M. Mr. Evans was administered a second thirty second jolt of electricity. The stench of burning flesh was nauseating. More smoke emanated from his leg and head. . . . At 8:40 P.M., a third charge of electricity thirty seconds in duration was passed through Mr. Evans' body. At 8:44 P.M. the doctors pronounced him dead. The execution of Mr. Evans took fourteen minutes.

This account is one in a long line of horrific executions by electrocution. In 1990, Jesse Tafero was killed by electrocution in Florida. He was still apparently breathing after the first two jolts of electricity coursed through his body. His head caught fire, literally burning him to death. Wayne Robert Felde was electrocuted in Louisiana in 1988. His head had been so badly burned that chunks of flesh had come off, revealing the skull bone. During Wilbert Evans' 1991 execution in Virginia, the media witnessed his body lunge forward as blood spurted from his nose and eyes. . . . In recent years, despite the Supreme Court's long-standing acquiescence in execution by electrocution, prisoners have challenged electrocution as cruel and unusual punishment. In 1999, the Court agreed to hear a constitutional challenge to Florida's use of the electric chair, thereby signaling the possibility that the Court might finally find the electric chair to be cruel and unusual punishment. But rather than defend its use of the electric chair, Florida joined the overwhelming majority of death penalty states by adopting lethal injection as its preferred method of execution. At present, there are only two states using the electric chair as their exclusive method of execution. . . .

> ## FAST FACT
>
> According to the Texas Department of Criminal Justice, the cost for the drugs used in lethal injection is $86.08.

Lethal Injection: The Modern Method of Execution

In 1977, Oklahoma became the first state to adopt the latest invention in the science of humane killing, the lethal injection machine. Just as the electric chair was invented as a modern and humane replacement for hanging, and the gas chamber was touted as more humane than the electric chair, so lethal injection has emerged as the humane execution method. In the United States, virtually all executions are now by lethal injection. All but two states have adopted lethal injection as the exclusive or preferred method of execution.

Lethal injection as a method of execution has become popular because it is perceived as a medical procedure. It has the appearance of being more "scientific" and "clinical" than electrocution or gassing. And since

Death penalty opponents in Alabama call on President Bush to put an end to capital punishment. Many opponents perceive execution as a form of legalized torture.

the prisoner is sedated before they are killed and there is no obvious damage to the prisoner's body from the process, the impression given is that they simply "go to sleep."

The equipment includes intravenous lines, prescription drugs, a hospital gurney and medical technicians. But of course, it is a medical procedure without a doctor—The American Medical Association has taken the position that it is a violation of medical ethics for a physician to participate in an execution in any way. . . .

In execution by lethal injection the prisoner is bound supine to a trolley and a trained nurse or technician injects the vein in the angle of the elbow. If the prisoner's veins are difficult to inject, or if she or he does not cooperate, or if there are problems [with collapsed veins] due to drug addiction, then the procedure becomes very difficult. After the cannula [a tube used to administer medication] has been passed successfully into the vein, three substances are injected: sodium thiopentone (a rapidly acting anesthetic), pancuronium bromide (a muscle relaxant to paralyze respiration) and potassium chloride (to stop the heart). The subject becomes unconscious within 10–15 seconds. Death is the result of anesthetic overdose as well as respiratory and cardiac arrest. The prisoner urinates and defecates, but the convulsions or spasms that would naturally occur are hidden by the first and second dosages of drugs that paralyze the prisoner.

A Legitimized Form of Torture

Though widely regarded as a painless and clean procedure, lethal injection also has a history of botches and human suffering. Texas has made full use of this humane and modern alternative to the electric chair and since 1977 has executed more people than any other state. The inventor of the lethal injection machine, Fred Leuchter, admitted that "about 80% of these [Texas] executions have had one problem or another. In the final analysis, it looks disgusting." The prisoners routinely choke, cough, spasm and writhe as they die.

In March 1984, James Autry was executed by lethal injection. It was reported that he took at least ten minutes to die and throughout much of that time was conscious and complaining of pain. In May 1989, an incorrect mix of lethal drugs caused Stephen McCoy to choke and heave throughout his execution. In December 1988, the intravenous

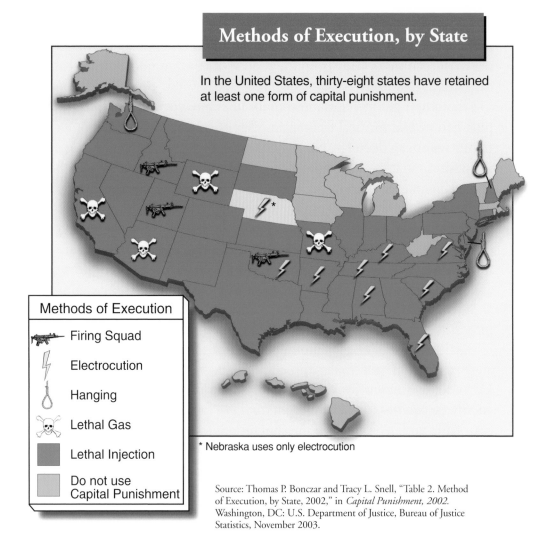

Methods of Execution, by State

In the United States, thirty-eight states have retained at least one form of capital punishment.

Methods of Execution

- Firing Squad
- Electrocution
- Hanging
- Lethal Gas
- Lethal Injection
- Do not use Capital Punishment

* Nebraska uses only electrocution

Source: Thomas P. Bonczar and Tracy L. Snell, "Table 2. Method of Execution, by State, 2002," in *Capital Punishment, 2002.* Washington, DC: U.S. Department of Justice, Bureau of Justice Statistics, November 2003.

line carrying a lethal injection into the arm of Raymond Landry sprang a leak, spraying technicians and witnesses with the fatal drugs. The tube had to be reinserted while Landry was half-dead. And in 1995, it took Virginia prison officers 40 minutes to insert the intravenous needle into the body of Richard Townes.

Given the problems with lethal injection, why has the method become the consensus method of execution in the United States? Don Cabana, a former death row prison warden answers: "The increasing use of the lethal injection as a means of capital punishment is nothing more than an attempt to sanitize the whole process. It makes society feel better to put a person to sleep than it does to electrocute or gas them. In some ways, I find lethal injection to be more objectionable and reprehensible than all the other methods. No matter how 'humane' an execution we devise, it is still a violation of human dignity." . . .

Like electrocution or gassing, death by lethal injection is nothing more than the latest technological innovation of a practice that will never be humane, painless, rapid or dignified. Capital punishment, whatever the method used, is, quite simply, a legitimized form of torture.

EVALUATING THE AUTHORS' ARGUMENTS:

In the viewpoint you just read, the authors contend that despite improvements in method, the execution of a prisoner constitutes torture. In the following viewpoint, the author charges that opponents of the death penalty have more compassion for murderers than they do for victims. After reading both viewpoints, which perspective do you find more convincing? Explain your reasoning.

The Death Penalty Is Not Cruel and Unusual Punishment

John O'Sullivan

> *"The death penalty is sometimes the only punishment that seems equal to the horror of a particular crime."*

In the following viewpoint, John O'Sullivan argues that the death penalty is a just response to crime. When one considers the nature of murder, especially violent and premeditated murder against children, the death penalty seems not to be cruel or unusual punishment, but a measured response to a heinous crime. Cruel and unusual punishments are those that exceed the nature of the crime; therefore, the author argues, if the state were to cut off a person's hand as punishment for a parking violation, this would constitute cruel and unusual punishment because it is unequal to the crime. Although critics complain that the death penalty is uncivilized, O'Sullivan points out that many civilized societies, such as Denmark and Norway, have reinstated the death penalty precisely to dole out appropriate sentences to those who have committed

John O'Sullivan, "Deadly Stakes: The Debate over Capital Punishment," *National Review Online*, August 20, 2002. Copyright © 2002 by the *National Review*. Reproduced by permission of United Feature Syndicate, Inc.

crimes against humanity. The author concludes by arguing that a society that sides with murderers over victims is uncivilized, and therefore the death penalty upholds civilization by protecting and honoring victims.

John O'Sullivan is an editor of *National Review,* a conservative journal from which this viewpoint was taken. His columns also appear in the *Chicago Sun-Times.*

AS YOU READ, CONSIDER THE FOLLOWING QUESTIONS:
1. According to the author, how does the opposition's support for life in prison undermine their argument that the death penalty is cruel and unusual punishment?
2. The author references Britain in the 1930s and America in the 1950s as examples of what?
3. According to O'Sullivan, what percent of the British public would like to see the death penalty reinstated?

By a terrible and macabre coincidence both the American and British peoples have found themselves confronted in the last few days with the chilling evil of child murder—and with the grave dilemma of exactly how to punish and deter it.

Last week a California jury found David Westerfield guilty of the kidnapping and murder of his neighbor's daughter, seven-year-old Danielle Van Dam, while in Britain the entire nation was convulsed for weeks over two missing ten-year-old girls. A nationwide hunt ended when their charred remains were found in a ditch. A school janitor has now been charged with their murders and, in a horrible echo of the "Moors Murders" four decades ago, his girlfriend is suspected of complicity in their deaths.

In both cases, it seems that the general public would like to see the death penalty imposed for these and similar crimes. If so, their wishes are almost certain to be thwarted by political elites.

Stubborn Opposition to the Death Penalty
In Britain this elite opposition is quite open. Though polls show that 82 percent of the British would like to see the death penalty

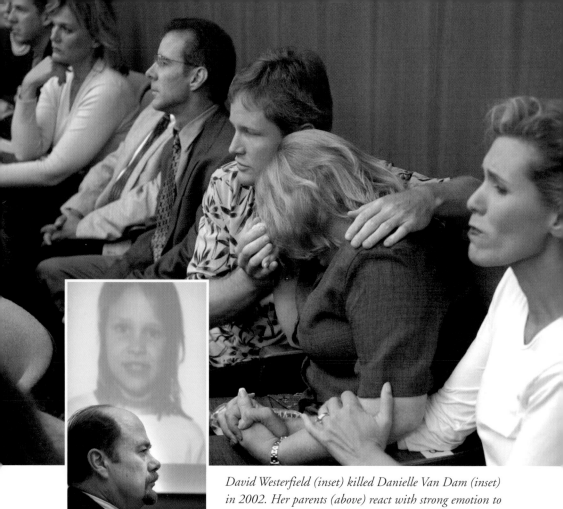

David Westerfield (inset) killed Danielle Van Dam (inset) in 2002. Her parents (above) react with strong emotion to his guilty verdict that carried the death penalty.

restored,[1] the politicians refuse to even discuss the matter. Their reluctance is reinforced by strong pressure from the European Union[2] that has decreed the death penalty to be incompatible with membership in its civilized ranks. Indeed, EU ambassadors troop annually to the [U.S.] State Department to protest the continued use of capital punishment in the U.S.—and the secretary of state replies apologetically that this is not really a matter for the federal government.

In California, the opposition is more subtle—perhaps because it is carried out in the obscurity of a tortuous appeals process. This is likely to ensure that even if Westerfield is sentenced to death [which he was in 2002], he will probably die of old age as courts endlessly debate his rights.

1. Britain abolished the death penalty for all crimes in 1998. 2. The European Union is an economic and political union of European nations.

Since this looks embarrassingly like an undemocratic contempt for majority opinion, opponents of capital punishment realize that they need formidable arguments to justify it. The arguments they use are as follows: that justifying the death penalty on the retributive grounds that the punishment should fit the crime is barbaric; that it does not deter potential murderers as its advocates claim; that there are no other arguments that might justify the state taking a life; that it risks killing the wrongly convicted; and, all in all, that it is a cruel punishment incompatible with a civilized society.

The Death Penalty Is Not Barbaric

Are these argument formidable? Well, they are repeated so frequently and in tones of such relentless moral self-congratulation that they doubtless come to seem formidable after a while. But they wilt upon examination. Let us take them in turn: Take retribution. This turns out to be a more complex argument than its opponents may have bargained for. To begin with, far from being cruel or barbaric, retribution is an argument that *limits* punishment as much as it extends it. We do not cut off hands for parking offenses even though that would undoubtedly halt such offenses overnight. Why? Because we recognize that it would violate retributive norms: It would be excessive in comparison to the crime and therefore cruel.

By the same logic, the death penalty is sometimes the only punishment that seems equal to the horror of a particular crime—a cold-blooded poisoning, say, or the rape and murder of a helpless child, or the mass murders [committed by] the Nazis and the Communists.

> ## FAST FACT
>
> According to a poll conducted by *Newsweek* in June 2000, 13 percent of those surveyed said they believe the death penalty provides comfort and consolation for victims' loved ones, while 26 percent said they believe the death penalty provides "eye for an eye" punishment for criminals.

Significantly, such civilized nations as the Danes and the Norwegians, which had abolished the death penalty before the First World War, restored it after 1945 in order to deal equitable justice to the Nazis and their collaborators. Was that an excessive response to millions of murders? Was it cruel, unusual, barbaric, uncivilized? Or a measured and just response to vast historic crimes?

Even abolitionists find it hard to reply to these questions because they differ among themselves about whether or not to stress the cruelty of the death penalty. Sometimes they assert that it is uniquely cruel; sometimes, however, they claim to favor lifetime imprisonment on the grounds that it is actually harsher than a quick trip to God or oblivion. Acting on the same grounds, retentionists [that is, supporters of the death penalty] can reasonably (and, I think, correctly) maintain that death is more merciful than lifetime incarceration (especially when that incarceration is accompanied by sadistic brutality from other inmates). . . .

The Death Penalty Is Compatible with Civilized Societies

Where, then, does that leave the final, broad conclusion that capital punishment is incompatible with a civilized society? Well, to answer that, we must have some idea of what abolitionists mean by "a civilized society."

Do they mean a society that has a written language, at least an oral historical tradition, social institutions that claim a monopoly of force and violence, and similar social inventions? It would seem not since such societies have almost invariably imposed the death penalty, sometimes for crimes much less serious than murder. Indeed, the replacement of private vendettas by state executions is as good a definition of the birth of civil society as political scientists can come up with.

Do they then mean a society marked by gentle manners, courtesy, low levels of private violence, and declining crime? If so, that argument too backfires on them. Britain in the 1930s and America in the 1950s were societies that had achieved high levels of social tranquility by comparison with their own pasts and the standards of other advanced societies. Yet they employed the death penalty for serious crimes—indeed, murder trials were among the gripping social entertainments of those days. And as the death penalty was gradually abolished (formal abolition generally following on a growing reluctance to impose it except in the most

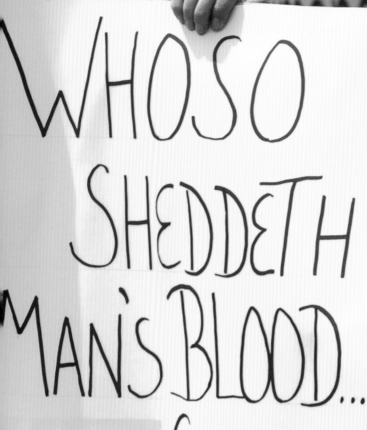

WHOSO SHEDDETH MAN'S BLOOD... GENESIS 9:6

MARYLAND
COALITION
FOR
STATE
EXECUTION

WWW.MC4SE.ORG

Some Americans, like this woman in Baltimore, believe that the Bible sanctions the death penalty.

David Westerfield listens as the court condemns him to death in 2002 for the murder of Danielle Van Dam.

terrible cases), so crime and violence rose, and so society became increasingly brutalist in its popular culture—the violence of films and television making the murder trials of the 1930s seem, well, civilized by comparison. . . .

What the "civilized" argument boils down to in the end, as the late [legal scholar] Ernest Van Den Haag used to point out in his intellectual demolitions of the abolitionist case, is the circular logic that capital punishment is incompatible with a civilized society because a civilized society is one that rejects capital punishment. Or, to put the abolitionist case as simply as possible: "People like us don't like capital punishment."

Pay More Attention to the Cries of Victims
A genuinely civilized society would take a very different view of the evidence cited above. It would pay more attention to the cries of the vic-

tims than to its own squeamishness. And it would transfer its compassion from the David Westerfields of this world to the Danielle Van Dams.

For if the death penalty would certainly have saved 820 innocent lives,[3] and might arguably save tens of thousands of innocent lives in the future, almost certainly at the cost of no innocent lives at all, then surely a society that shrinks from using it deserves to be called sentimentalist and cruel rather than civilized. And if in addition it ignores majority opinion in order to indulge its refined sensibilities, then it deserves to be called undemocratic too.

EVALUATING THE AUTHORS' ARGUMENTS:

In the viewpoint you just read, the author contends that the death penalty is compatible with civilized societies. The authors of the previous article argue that it is uncivilized to execute people, however. In your opinion, which authors' argument is more compelling? Explain your answer.

3. The author is referring to 820 people who were killed by murderers who had repeatedly killed. His point is that if the murderers had been executed after their first murder, then 820 people would still be alive.

VIEWPOINT 5

Juveniles Should Receive the Death Penalty

Paul Rosenzweig

"It makes no sense to say such conduct is categorically ineligible for the death penalty."

In the following viewpoint, Paul Rosenzweig argues that juveniles who commit capital crimes should be eligible to receive the death penalty. He suggests that juveniles know that murder is wrong, and are therefore just as culpable for their actions as adults are. Moreover, the author points out that little emotional or developmental difference exists between someone who is seventeen and a half years old and someone who is eighteen; therefore, the line separating juvenile crimes from adult crimes is arbitrary and meaningless. Rosenzweig concludes that juveniles should remain eligible to receive the death penalty because it is in line with the principles of capital punishment.

In addition to being a professor of law at George Mason University School of Law, Paul Rosenzweig is a senior legal research fellow at the Heritage Foundation, a conservative think tank.

AS YOU READ, CONSIDER THE FOLLOWING QUESTIONS:

1. How does the author characterize the 2002 sniper shootings?
2. According to the author, what is different about drinking, driving, voting, and committing murder?
3. How old was John Lee Malvo when he was arrested?

Paul Rosenzweig, "For Adults Only?" *The Washington Times,* November 14, 2002, p. A20. Copyright © 2002 by *The Washington Times.* All rights reserved. Reproduced by permission.

S hould juvenile convicts be spared the death penalty, no matter how heinous their crimes? A sizable minority of justices on the U.S. Supreme Court says yes.

In a recent dissent, four justices argued that, in all circumstances, the execution of a convict under the age of 18 at the time he committed murder is unconstitutional. Their reasoning: Given their youth, juvenile offenders aren't as morally responsible as adults. Juveniles lack "the same capacity to control their conduct and think in long-range terms" as adults, they wrote.

Thus, according to the justices, it is never permissible to execute someone who committed a crime while under the age of 18. The *New York Times* agreed, calling the execution of juvenile offenders a disgrace.

One wonders what they would say today. Two days after the court opinion was issued (and a few hours after the *Times* editorial was finalized for publication), John Allen Muhammad [41 years old] and John Lee Malvo [17 years old] were arrested. It appears both will be charged with multiple counts of murder relating to the string of sniper homicides in the Washington metropolitan area [in the fall of 2002].

(Inset) A bouquet and a bullet hole mark the site of one of ten murders committed by Muhammad and Malvo who shot their victims from their car (below).

The initial evidence gathered by the police makes it clear the sniper attacks were chillingly premeditated and deliberate. The sniper had a tripod and scope for firing the rifle. The car Mr. Muhammad and Mr. Malvo were driving had been modified to allow the sniper to lie down in the trunk and shoot his victims through a hole in the back of the car, making escape that much easier. In short, the sniper hunted human beings as if they were deer in a forest, with as much care and forethought as a military battle planner.

An Arbitrary Bright Line

Now, Mr. Muhammad and Mr. Malvo are innocent until proven guilty. But let's engage in a thought experiment and assume the two are convicted of these horrendous crimes. The initial assumption of investigators appeared to be that Mr. Muhammad was the shooter and Mr. Malvo drove the getaway car. But legally, the getaway driver for a serial murderer is as guilty of the crime as the shooter himself. If the driver were 25 years old, many juries likely would sen-

John Lee Malvo, a minor, was charged with multiple counts of premeditated murder in the Washington sniper case.

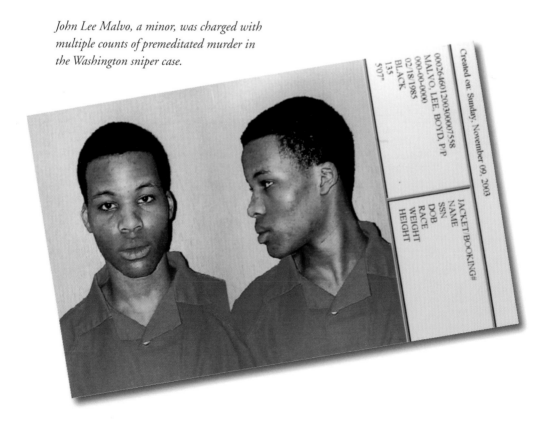

tence him to death, even though his role was merely that of an accomplice.

Still, the driver's somewhat lesser role in the crime does make it possible a jury might show mercy and recommend that he not be sentenced to death. And that recommendation is made more likely by virtue of Mr. Malvo's youth—a jury may not want to sentence a 17-year-old accomplice to death.

But let's turn the picture around and modify our thought experiment.

What if the evidence proves Mr. Malvo was the shooter or, as some investigators believe, that he and Mr. Muhammad took turns hunting humans?

What if it were a 17-year-old who planned and executed each murder alone? Surely a jury wouldn't decline to impose the death penalty simply because he's several months short of his 18th birthday. To do so would mean drawing an arbitrary bright line between the acts of an individual who's 17 years and 6 months old and one who's 18.

Juveniles Know That Murder Is Wrong

But, critics reply, there are many instances in which the law draws bright lines based upon age. Yet it's wrong to think that only with the maturity necessary to drive carefully, drink responsibly, and vote intelligently does one come to understand that murdering another human being is wrong. That kind of understanding comes at a much younger age.

Besides, we determine the guilt or innocence of any defendant on an individual basis. Laws governing driving, drinking and voting represent gross generalizations—appropriate in making broad public policy but utterly inconsistent with our concept of individual criminal responsibility.

The absurdity of the position taken by [those opposed to executing child offenders] is only heightened by the arrests made in the sniper case. Their reasoning boils down to this: A juvenile should never be punished

As a juvenile, seventeen-year-old serial killer John Lee Malvo was sentenced to life in prison. Many argued that he deserved to die despite his young age.

in proportion to his crime because he always lacks culpable moral responsibility. But if the evidence at Mr. Malvo's trial proves what most people suspect, there can be little doubt as to moral culpability. Either as driver or shooter, Mr. Malvo apparently acted as a knowing participant in a string of coldblooded murders. It makes no sense to say such conduct is categorically ineligible for the death penalty.

EVALUATING THE AUTHORS' ARGUMENTS:

In the viewpoint you just read, the author argues that John Lee Malvo should be eligible for the death penalty because he committed cold-blooded murder. In the following viewpoint, the author argues that juveniles such as Malvo should not receive the death penalty because juveniles ought not be held to the same judicial standards as adults. After reading both viewpoints, do you think that juveniles and adults should be held to equal standards in a court of law? Why or why not? Explain your answer.

Juveniles Should Not Receive the Death Penalty

Anthony M. Kennedy

> *"Differences between juvenile and adult offenders are too . . . well understood to risk allowing a youthful person to receive the death penalty."*

In the following viewpoint, Supreme Court justice Anthony M. Kennedy explains why the Supreme Court on March 1, 2005, decreed it unconstitutional to sentence juvenile offenders to death. Kennedy argues that juvenile offenders should be ineligible for the death penalty because they committed their crime when they were immature, impetuous, and lacked the foresight to appreciate the long-term consequences of their actions. In addition, as juveniles they were susceptible to powerful peer pressure and outside influences, further damaging their sense of propriety. Finally, Justice Kennedy argues that juvenile offenders have a better chance of being rehabilitated than do adult criminals and thus should be spared the death penalty.

Justice Anthony M. Kennedy has sat on the Supreme Court since his appointment by President Ronald Reagan in 1988.

Anthony M. Kennedy, majority opinion, *Roper v. Simmons,* Washington, DC, March 1, 2005.

AS YOU READ, CONSIDER THE FOLLOWING QUESTIONS:
1. According to Justice Kennedy, what deterrent effect does the death penalty have on juvenile offenders?
2. Why is it important to the author's argument to question whether a juvenile offender is the worst type of offender?
3. According to Justice Kennedy, why are the crimes of juveniles not as morally reprehensible as those of adults?

At the age of 17, when he was still a junior in high school, Christopher Simmons, the respondent here, committed murder. About nine months later, after he had turned 18, he was tried and sentenced to death. There is little doubt that Simmons was the instigator of the crime. Before its commission Simmons said he wanted to murder someone. In chilling, callous terms he talked about his plan, discussing it for the most part with two friends, Charles Benjamin and John Tessmer, then aged 15 and 16, respectively. Simmons proposed to commit burglary and murder by breaking and entering, tying up a victim, and throwing the victim off a bridge. . . .

The State [of Missouri] charged Simmons with burglary, kidnaping, stealing, and murder in the first degree. As Simmons was 17 at the time of the crime, he was outside the criminal jurisdiction of Missouri's juvenile court system. He was tried as an adult. At trial the State introduced Simmons' confession and the videotaped reenactment of the crime, along with testimony that Simmons discussed the crime in advance and bragged about it later. The defense called no witnesses in the guilt phase. The jury having returned a verdict of murder, the trial proceeded to the penalty phase. The State sought the death penalty. . . .

Juveniles Are Ineligible for the Death Penalty

A majority of States have rejected the imposition of the death penalty on juvenile offenders under 18, and we now hold this is required by the Eighth Amendment.

Because the death penalty is the most severe punishment, the Eighth Amendment applies to it with special force. . . . These rules vindicate the underlying principle that the death penalty is reserved for a narrow category of crimes and offenders.

Three general differences between juveniles under 18 and adults demonstrate that juvenile offenders cannot with reliability be classified among the worst offenders. First, as any parent knows and as the scientific and sociological studies respondent and his *amici* [friends of the court] cite tend to confirm, "[a] lack of maturity and an underdeveloped sense of responsibility are found in youth more often than in adults and are more understandable among the young. These qualities often result in impetuous and ill-considered actions and decisions." It has been noted that "adolescents are overrepresented

Christopher Simmons committed murder as a minor. In March 2005 the Supreme Court ruled that because of Simmons's age at the time of the crime he was not eligible for the death penalty.

statistically in virtually every category of reckless behavior." In recognition of the comparative immaturity and irresponsibility of juveniles, almost every State prohibits those under 18 years of age from voting, serving on juries, or marrying without parental consent.

The second area of difference is that juveniles are more vulnerable or susceptible to negative influences and outside pressures, including peer pressure. This is explained in part by the prevailing circumstance that juveniles have less control, or less experience with control, over their own environment.

The third broad difference is that the character of a juvenile is not as well formed as that of an adult. The personality traits of juveniles are more transitory, less fixed.

These differences render suspect any conclusion that a juvenile falls among the worst offenders. The susceptibility of juveniles to immature

In October 2004 people line up to enter the U.S. Supreme Court to hear the ruling on the constitutionality of executing juveniles. The judges ruled that juvenile executions are unconstitutional.

Source: Sargent. © 1993 by Universal Press Syndicate. Reproduced by permission.

and irresponsible behavior means "their irresponsible conduct is not as morally reprehensible as that of an adult." Their own vulnerability and comparative lack of control over their immediate surroundings mean juveniles have a greater claim than adults to be forgiven for failing to escape negative influences in their whole environment. The reality that juveniles still struggle to define their identity means it is less supportable to conclude that even a heinous crime committed by a juvenile is evidence of irretrievably depraved character. From a moral standpoint it would be misguided to equate the failings of a minor with those of an adult, for a greater possibility exists that a minor's character deficiencies will be reformed. Indeed, "[t]he relevance of youth as a mitigating factor derives from the fact that the signature qualities of youth are transient; as individuals mature, the impetuousness and recklessness that may dominate in younger years can subside." . . .

Immaturity, Vulnerability, and Lack of True Depravity

As for deterrence, it is unclear whether the death penalty has a significant or even measurable deterrent effect on juveniles. . . . The absence of evidence of deterrent effect is of special concern because the same characteristics that render juveniles less culpable than adults suggest as well that juveniles will be less susceptible to deterrence. In particular, as the plurality observed in *Thompson* [an earlier case], "[t]he likelihood that the teenage offender has made the kind of cost-benefit analysis that attaches any weight to the possibility of execution is so remote as to be virtually nonexistent." To the extent the juvenile death penalty might have residual deterrent effect, it is worth noting that the punishment of life imprisonment without the possibility of parole is itself a severe sanction, in particular for a young person. . . .

The differences between juvenile and adult offenders are too marked and well understood to risk allowing a youthful person to receive the death penalty despite insufficient culpability. An unacceptable likelihood exists that the brutality or cold-blooded nature of any particular crime would overpower mitigating arguments based on youth as a matter of course, even where the juvenile offender's objective immaturity, vulnerability, and lack of true depravity should require a sentence less severe than death.

EVALUATING THE AUTHORS' ARGUMENTS:

In the viewpoints you just read, the authors disagree over whether juveniles who commit crimes are as culpable for their actions as adults. After reading both articles, what is your position on this issue? Explain your thinking.

CHAPTER 2

Is the Death Penalty Effective?

A death row inmate in a Texas prison stares out at an empty hall from behind bars.

VIEWPOINT 1

The Death Penalty Deters Crime

Jeff Jacoby

"Murder becomes more attractive when potential killers know that prison is the worst outcome they can face."

In the following viewpoint, Jeff Jacoby argues that the presence of the death penalty curbs murder in the United States. He cites statistics that suggest the period during which there was no death penalty murder rates went up, and when the death penalty was reinstated murder rates dropped. Moreover, he provides data that shows that the states that conduct the most executions have the lowest murder rate. If there are problems with the death penalty system, Jacoby suggests fixing them rather than discarding it completely. He concludes that the death penalty protects against the murder of innocent people and should be retained as a just and effective punishment for crime.

Jeff Jacoby is a columnist for the *Boston Globe,* from which this viewpoint was taken.

AS YOU READ, CONSIDER THE FOLLOWING QUESTIONS:
1. What was the murder rate in Texas in 1991?
2. During what years was there no death penalty in the United States?
3. According to the author, what is the problem with establishing a moratorium on the death penalty?

Jeff Jacoby, "Capital Punishment Saves Lives," *The Boston Globe,* June 6, 2002. Copyright © 2002 by *The Boston Globe.* Reproduced by permission of Copyright Clearance Center, Inc.

Death penalty abolitionists don't usually mention it, but in promoting a moratorium on executions, they are urging us down a road we have taken before.

In the mid-1960s, as a number of legal challenges to capital punishment began working their way through the courts, executions in the United States came to a halt. From 56 in 1960, the number of killers put to death dropped to seven in 1965, to one in 1966, and to zero in 1967. There it stayed for the next 10 years, until the State of Utah executed Gary Gilmore in 1977. That was the only execution in 1977, and there were only two more during the next three years.

Gary Gilmore was the only person to be executed in the United States in 1977.

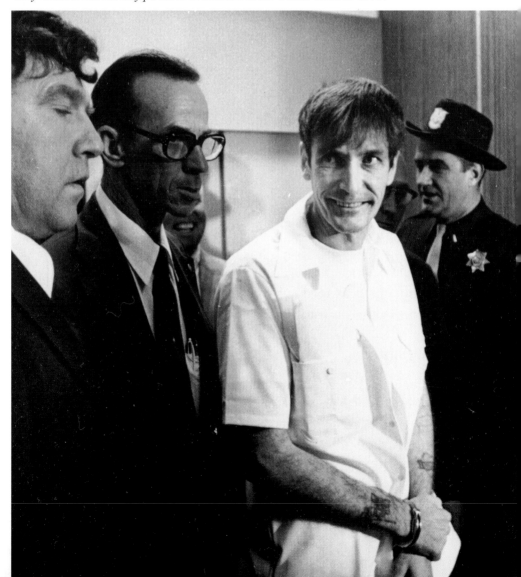

Without the Death Penalty, Murders "Skyrocket"

In sum, between 1965 and 1980, there was practically no death penalty in the United States, and for 10 of those 16 years—1967–76—there was *literally* no death penalty: a national moratorium.

What was the effect of making capital punishment unavailable for a decade and a half? Did a moratorium on executions save innocent lives—or cost them?

The data are brutal. Between 1965 and 1980, annual murders in the United States skyrocketed, rising from 9,960 to 23,040. The murder rate—homicides per 100,000 persons—doubled from 5.1 to 10.2.

Was it just a fluke that the steepest increase in murder in US history coincided with the years when the death penalty was not available to punish it? Perhaps. Or perhaps murder becomes more attractive when potential killers know that prison is the worst outcome they can face.

FAST FACT

The National Center for Policy Analysis claims that every execution results in eighteen fewer murders.

By contrast, common sense suggests that there are at least some people who will *not* commit murder if they think it might cost them their lives. Sure enough, as executions have become more numerous, murder has declined. "From 1995 to 2000," notes Dudley Sharp of the victims rights group Justice For All, "executions averaged 71 per year, a 21,000 percent increase over the 1966–1980 period. The murder rate dropped from a high of 10.2 (per 100,000) in 1980 to 5.7 in 1999—a 44 percent reduction. The murder rate is now at its lowest level since 1966."

The More Executions, the Less Homicide

What is true nationally has been observed locally as well. There were 12,652 homicides in New York during the 25 years from 1940 to 1965, when New York regularly executed murderers. By contrast, during the 25 years from 1966 to 1991 there were no executions at all—and murders quadrupled to 51,638.

To be sure, murder rates fell in almost every state in the 1990s. But they fell the most in states that use capital punishment. The most strik-

Luis Vasquez stands as the judge sentences him to life in prison for the kidnapping, rape, and murder of a Boston woman in 2001.

ing protection of innocent life has been in Texas, which executes more murderers than any other state. In 1991, the Texas murder rate was 15.3 per 100,000. By 1999, it had fallen to 6.1—a drop of 60 percent. Within Texas, the most aggressive death penalty prosecutions are in Harris County (the Houston area). Since the resumption of executions in 1982, the annual number of Harris County murders has plummeted from 701 to 241—a 72 percent decrease.

Obviously, murder and the rate at which it occurs are affected by more than just the presence or absence of the death penalty. But even after taking that caveat into account, it seems irrefutably clear that when murderers are executed, innocent lives are saved. And when executions are stopped, innocent lives are lost.

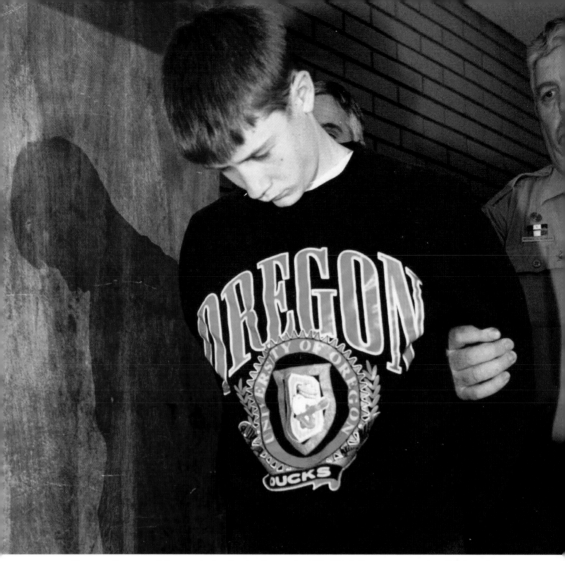

Because the state of Oregon lacks the death penalty, Kip Kinkel was sentenced to life in prison for killing his parents and fellow students during a 1998 shooting spree.

Gravestones Across the Land

Death penalty abolitionists (and a few death penalty supporters) claim that a moratorium on executions is warranted because the criminal justice system is "broken" and the death penalty is unfairly applied. But if that's true when the punishment is death, how much more so is it true when the punishment isn't death! Death penalty prosecutions typically undergo years of appeals, often attracting intense scrutiny and media attention. So painstaking is the super–due process[1] of capital murder cases that for all the recent hype about innocent prisoners on death row,

1. Due process is the established course for judicial proceedings designed to protect an individual's legal rights.

there is not a single proven case in modern times of an innocent person being executed in the United States.

But the due process in non-death penalty cases is not nearly as scrupulous. Everyone knows that there are innocent people behind bars today. If the legal system's flaws justify a moratorium on capital punishment, *a fortiori* [it stands to reason that] they justify a moratorium on imprisonment. Those who call for a moratorium on executions should be calling just as vehemently for a moratorium on prison terms. Why don't they?

Because they know how ridiculous it would sound. If there are problems with the system, the system should be fixed, but refusing to punish criminals would succeed only in making society far less safe than it is today.

The same would be true of a moratorium on executions. If due process in capital murder cases can be made even more watertight, by all means let us do so. But not by keeping the worst of our murderers alive until perfection is achieved. We've been down the moratorium road before. We know how that experiment turns out. The results are written in wrenching detail on gravestones across the land.

EVALUATING THE AUTHORS' ARGUMENTS:

In the viewpoint you just read, the author relies heavily on statistics and data to make his point. In the following viewpoint, the author relies heavily on reasoning and example to make his point. In your opinion, do these differences affect the persuasiveness of either argument? If so, in what way?

The Death Penalty Does Not Deter Crime

Marshall Dayan

"'You can tell people that you're going to boil 'em in hot oil, but it won't deter crime.'"

In the following viewpoint, Marshall Dayan argues that the death penalty is not a deterrent to murder because criminals do not expect to be caught. He reasons that this indicates murderers do not take into account the punishment associated with their crime before they commit it, and so the punishment had no effect on their decision to kill. The author suggests that the only way the death penalty might serve as a deterrent is if a person who is well versed in the severity of the death penalty were to refrain from committing a crime based on their knowledge of it. He raises the case of William G. Huggins Jr., a former district attorney who was prosecuted on murder charges. The author concludes that because Huggins was very familiar with capital punishment but committed murder anyway, the death penalty does not prevent anyone from committing crimes.

Marshall Dayan is an assistant professor of law at North Carolina Central University. In 1998 he was awarded the Paul Green Award of the North Carolina American Civil Liberties Union and the Paul Green Foundation for his efforts to abolish the death penalty in North Carolina.

AS YOU READ, CONSIDER THE FOLLOWING QUESTIONS:
1. What type of person did Justice Brennan describe to be "implausible"?
2. According to Dayan, what significance is it that William G. Huggins knew how frequently the death penalty was sought in his county?
3. According to the author, the death penalty is no more of a deterrent to murder than what other punishment?

How often have we heard politicians, prosecutors and others insist that we as a society must impose the death penalty for the crime of murder because it will certainly deter others from committing a similar crime? It is a familiar refrain, and we hear it even more lately as a defense to those who propose that a moratorium on the death penalty is necessary to attempt to fix the numerous problems plaguing application of the death penalty—the shocking number of innocent people sentenced to death, questions of race and class discrimination, the uneven and arbitrary quality of counsel, the politics of the judiciary presiding over capital trials and appeals, and the absence of narrow guidelines for who might be eligible for this most severe punishment. Yet, a recent news event here in North Carolina has once again called into question whether even the death penalty can actually deter crime.

FAST FACT

According to the Death Penalty Information Center, the death penalty does not deter murderers from killing. North Dakota, Maine, Rhode Island, and Minnesota—all states that have abolished the death penalty—have lower murder rates than do Alabama, Tennessee, Illinois, and Maryland, all states that employ the death penalty.

Criminals Do Not Expect to Get Caught

Among the main purposes of punishment for crime are deterrence, prevention, rehabilitation, and retribution. Of these four, deterrence is considered the most important, because theoretically, it can have the greatest effect on society at large. Numerous social science studies, however, have called into question whether the death penalty is any more effective at deterring crime than is imprisonment for life.

A condemned prisoner is led to California's San Quentin State Prison's death row. Some statistics show that the death penalty does not deter murderers.

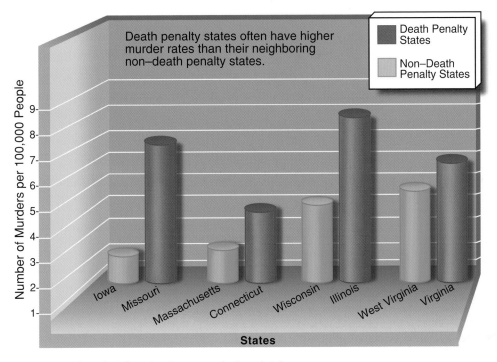

Death penalty states often have higher murder rates than their neighboring non–death penalty states.

Source: Death Penalty Information Center, www.deathpenaltyinfo.org.

In spite of these studies, prosecutors regularly justify the use of the death penalty by insisting that the death penalty does deter crime. Others argue that no criminal punishment can deter very much, not even the death penalty, because for deterrence to work, the potential criminal must think about the consequences. A former client of mine, a convicted murderer once said, "You can tell people that you're going to boil 'em in hot oil, but it won't deter crime because criminals don't think they're going to get caught." Similarly, [Supreme Court] Justice William Brennan wrote, "It is not denied that many, and probably most, capital crimes cannot be deterred by the threat of punishment. Thus the argument can apply only to those who think rationally about the commission of capital crimes. Particularly is that true when the potential criminal, under this argument, must not only consider the risk of punishment, but also distinguish between two possible punishments. The concern, then, is with a particular type of potential criminal, the rational person who will commit a

The death penalty failed to deter attorney William G. Huggins from plotting to kill his wife in 2002.

capital crime knowing that the punishment is long-term imprisonment, which may well be for the rest of his life, but will not commit the crime knowing that the punishment is death. On the face of it, the assumption that such persons exist is implausible."

If It Did Not Deter a Prosecutor, It Will Not Deter Anyone

While Justice Brennan is probably right that no such person exists, it is possible to think of who such a person might be. The criminal subject to deterrence surely would know that the death penalty could be applied for his crime if he were to be caught, and would therefore have to have some legal knowledge. This person would also know the likelihood of being caught, and would therefore have to have some knowledge of law enforcement. In short, the person most likely to be deterred by the threat of the death penalty would be a prosecutor, a District Attorney or Assistant District Attorney.

[In September 2002] Assistant District Attorney William G. Huggins, Jr. of the 11A Judicial District, Lee County, was arrested on charges of solicitation of murder [that is, hiring a person to kill someone else]. If the murder had taken place, Huggins could have been convicted for acting in concert to commit first degree murder or accessory before the fact to first degree murder, either of which could carry the death penalty. This week, a Lee County District Court Judge found probable cause to believe that the crime of solicitation had been committed, and bound the case over to the Superior Court. If anyone could be deterred by the threat of the death penalty, it would be a prosecutor. In particular, it would be an Assistant District Attorney in the 11A prosecutorial district. The elected District Attorney, Thomas Lock, has frequently sought the death penalty in this prosecutorial district, so the death penalty is in no way foreign to William Huggins. Yet if the allegations are true, Huggins was undeterred. Those who argue that the death penalty has a deterrent effect simply haven't heard about William G. Huggins, Jr.

EVALUATING THE AUTHORS' ARGUMENTS:

In order to make their argument, both Marshall Dayan and Jeff Jacoby consider whether or not a potential murderer is likely to consider the consequences of their actions prior to committing a crime. After reading both viewpoints, whose conclusion do you find most persuasive, and why? Explain your reasoning.

VIEWPOINT 3

The Death Penalty Saves Innocent Lives

Don Feder

In the following viewpoint, Don Feder argues that executing murderers spares the lives of the victims they would have killed had they remained alive. He contends that if they do not receive the death penalty, most murderers will eventually be released from prison, upon which point they are likely to kill again. In addition to these repeat victims, the author argues that in general, the threat of the death penalty discourages people from committing murder, and so this is another way in which the death penalty works to protect innocent people from being murdered. Feder concludes by arguing that opponents of the death penalty have misplaced their sympathies with murderers rather than innocents, and that murderers deserve to meet the same fate that they cruelly imposed on their victims.

Don Feder's columns appear in the *Boston Herald, Human Events,* and *Jewish World Review,* from which this viewpoint was taken. He is also the author of *Who Is Afraid of the Religious Right?* and *A Jewish Conservative Looks at Pagan America.*

> *"When murderers aren't executed, innocents suffer."*

AS YOU READ, CONSIDER THE FOLLOWING QUESTIONS:
1. According to the author, what effect has reinstating the death penalty had?
2. What does Feder mean when he states that fifteen thousand innocents are dying every year in America?
3. How many people died in the April 1995 bombing of the Alfred P. Murrah building in Oklahoma City?

Jesse Jackson—who regularly substitutes rhymes for reason—was in Oklahoma [in January 2001] as part of his nationwide anti–death penalty tour.

The state is set to execute eight people [in January 2001] which has the misplaced-compassion crowd in a tizzy. "Oklahoma must choose to stop the death machine," Jesse told 500 people at the Fairview Baptist Church in Oklahoma City.

In June 2000 the state of Texas executed Gary Graham for the 1981 murder of Bobby Lambert.

Jackson is on the road again, bemoaning the fate of killers. In June [2000], he witnessed the execution of Texas inmate Gary Graham, proclaiming him "an innocent martyr."

Morgan Reynolds, head of the Criminal Justice Center of the National Center for Policy Analysis, considers Graham an unlikely poster child for anti–death penalty forces.

Among other incontrovertible evidence, there was an eyewitness to Graham's 1981 murder of Bobby Lambert. A deputy sheriff testified the martyr-to-be told him, "Next time, I'm not going to leave any witnesses."

The murder for which this gentle soul was sent into the great beyond was part of a crime spree that included four shootings, 10 armed robberies and a rape. (One of Graham's other victims said he told her, "I've killed three people, and I'm going to kill you.") State and federal courts turned down more than 40 of his appeals. Graham might be innocent. The Easter Bunny might have pulled the trigger. One is as probable as the other.

Living Murderers Will Kill Again

But the possibility of executing an innocent is the big gun of death penalty opponents. In this country, it takes roughly 11 years to pull the switch on a convicted murderer, more than enough time to test the original verdict, examine every scintilla of evidence and apply foolproof forensic procedures like DNA testing.

Despite all of this, it must be admitted that an innocent person can be executed. But innocents are already dying, at the rate of about 15,000 a year in America.

When murderers aren't executed, innocents suffer. Odds are a killer will be released at some point. And there's a fair chance that he or she will

In 2000 George W. Bush, then-governor of Texas, addresses the press after the execution of Gary Graham. Bush firmly believed that justice had been served.

kill again. In fact, there's a far greater likelihood of this than of an innocent man taking that long walk [down death row and being executed].

The Death Penalty Prevents Murder

Opponents argue that deterrence is a myth. How do they know? Survey takers don't go around asking, "Were you ever deterred from killing someone by the possibility that you might pay the ultimate price?"

Still, a cause and effect may be surmised.

Since 1973, when the death penalty was reimposed, we've had more than 660 executions nationwide. In 1999, the murder rate was the lowest since 1966 (5.7 per 100,000). Coincidence? [In 2000] Texas had half the executions in America. President George [W.] Bush is

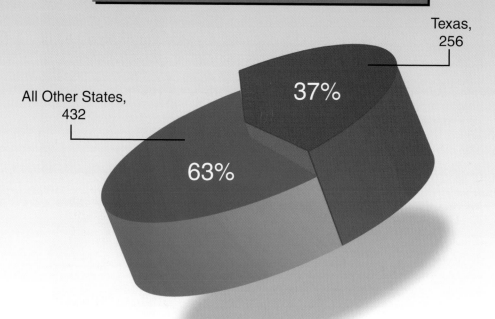

Texas,
256

All Other States,
432

37%

63%

Source: "Executions in the United States from 1993 to 2003 (as of October 1, 2003)," in *Executions in the United States.* Washington, DC: Death Penalty Information Center, 2003.

still berated for presiding over more executions [when he was governor of Texas] than any other governor.

The county that includes Houston has the most executions in the state. Between 1982, when executions were resumed in Texas, and 1996, Houston's homicide rate fell 63 percent. In the same period, the national homicide rate declined by 19 percent. Coincidence again? . . .

Have Sympathy for Victims, Not Murderers

Will Jackson hold church rallies before the executions of the white supremacists who murdered James Byrd in 1998? Will he shed public tears for the monsters who dragged Byrd more than two miles behind their pickup truck, until his head and one limb were torn from his body?

[In December 2000] a federal judge in Denver granted [Oklahoma City bomber] Timothy McVeigh's petition to end attempts to stay his execution. A date for McVeigh's death can be set by the director of the federal Bureau of Prisons any time after January 11 [2001].[1]

1. McVeigh was executed on June 11, 2001.

McVeigh was convicted of the murders of 168 people in the [April 19] 1995 bombing of the Alfred P. Murrah federal building in Oklahoma City.

What do you think, Jesse? Is McVeigh an innocent martyr? Did he have adequate counsel? Are a disproportionate number of white militia-types being executed in America?

McVeigh ran his own private death machine. Unlike the death-row population, those who died that April day did not deserve their fate. Opponents of the death penalty never talk about such innocents. And if they care about them at all, you wouldn't know it.

> **EVALUATING THE AUTHORS' ARGUMENTS:**
>
> In the viewpoint you just read, the author argues that murderers who are not executed are likely to be released from prison and murder again. In the following viewpoint, Nicolai Brown argues that murderers who spend the bulk of their lives in prison pose no further threat to society. Which argument do you find more persuasive, and why? Explain your reasoning.

The Death Penalty Encourages Violence

Nicolai Brown

"Our government sends the message that killing people is, in fact, an acceptable way to deal with problems."

In the following viewpoint, Nicolai Brown argues that the death penalty should be abolished because it encourages murder and violence. Capital punishment constitutes an excessive use of force, which the author argues is criminal. Once criminals are put in prison they no longer pose a danger to society, so executing them is an act of unnecessary and illegal force. Brown suggests that the reason the United States has the highest murder rate of all industrialized nations is because the government, by engaging in state-sponsored killings, sends the message that murder is acceptable. He concludes it is hypocritical for the United States to use murder to attempt to prevent murder.

Nicolai Brown is a columnist for the *Iowa State Daily*, the newspaper of Iowa State University.

1. What right do individuals have when attacked, according to the author?
2. What punishments does Brown believe are appropriate for minor crimes and major crimes?
3. According to the author, what does the United States have in common with China, Iran, and North Korea?

The practice of lethal injection was challenged in a federal court in Columbus, Ohio [in June 2004]. The lawsuit, filed on behalf of death row inmates Adremy Dennis and Richard Cooey, alleges that the particular use of chemicals causes unseen torturous pain in its recipients—thus violating the Eighth Amendment. Regardless of the validity of the lawyers' claim, their case brings to light the question of necessity regarding our use of capital punishment.

Is capital punishment necessary to protect society from our most heinous criminals? An examination of the issue clearly shows it is not only unnecessary, but hypocritical in making a statement against killing people by turning around and, well, killing people.

Self-Defense and the Use of Force

Necessity is the defining element of self-defense. When faced with a physical threat, individuals have the right to protect themselves using whatever means are available, so long as those means don't cross the line of excess.

For example, an individual confronted by someone who seeks to physically harm him or her has the right to put down the attacker by using the minimal means necessary to safely stop the attack—be it via threat or warning, "hand to hand" defense or the use of weapons. Every situation differs because the people involved, their personal circumstances, and available means of protection are never quite the same. The point of self-defense is to stop an attack while retaining moral high ground. Once the threat of attack is gone, further action is no longer considered self-defense.

Source: Engelhardt. © 1993 by the *St. Louis Post-Dispatch*. Reproduced by permission.

Continued violence against an attacker may be explained by the heat of the moment, but not excused. In other words, excessive use of force is not defensive, but criminal.

This line of reasoning is extended from the individual to society through our use of jails and prisons to protect ourselves from all sorts of criminals. Those deemed to represent a relatively minor danger to others are typically sent to minimum security institutions where they spend shorter amounts of time incarcerated.

Little Other than Judicial Murder

It makes sense: minor punishments for minor crimes. Conversely, major crimes such as rape and murder warrant longer sentences carried out in more closely controlled environments.

Again, the logic adds up: major sentences for major crimes. In all cases, the sentence handed down is intended to fit the crime by protecting society proportional to the threat posed by the convicted individual.

Capital punishment falls outside of this model. By choosing to end the life of an individual in its custody, the state rejects the principles of self-defense in favor of using unnecessary force to subdue a threat. Once a person is found guilty and sent to prison, he or she no longer represent a threat to society.

Missouri residents demonstrate against their state's death penalty in 1999 on the grounds that the death penalty inspires violence by example.

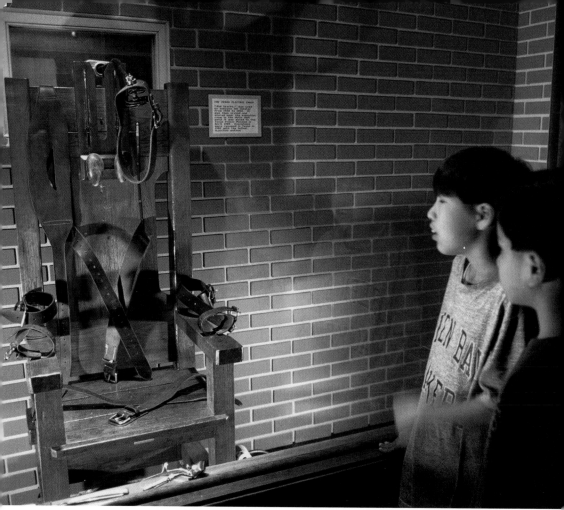

Texas elementary school students view an electric chair in a museum. Controversy exists over whether the death penalty encourages violence among America's youth.

Even if that person's future release is deemed out of the question, capital punishment is still unnecessary because another effective solution, life imprisonment, exists. Therefore, capital punishment crosses the line of excess whereby the state can no longer claim moral high ground. It amounts to little other than judicial murder.

The Death Penalty Condones Murder

Rather than exacting excessive punishment through the death penalty, our government should abolish its use, as have virtually all other industrialized nations. In leading by example, our government would send a clear and strong message to citizens that killing people isn't an acceptable way of dealing with our problems.

By contrast, our government sends the message that killing people is, in fact, an acceptable way to deal with problems. Perhaps this is why the United States has (by far) the highest murder rate of all industrialized nations.

The government should not be in the business of killing people. Our use of capital punishment puts us among nations such as China, Iran and North Korea in terms of the number of human beings judicially murdered. That's some pretty bad company.

It's time to join the 21st century and abolish capital punishment.

EVALUATING THE AUTHOR'S ARGUMENTS:

In the viewpoint you just read, the author suggests that the death penalty encourages murder because people are likely to follow the example of the government. After reading the article, carefully consider this claim. Do you think it is true that citizens look to the government for a model of behavior? In your opinion, should the government conduct itself the way it wants its citizens to? Why or why not?

CHAPTER 3

Is the Death Penalty Applied Fairly?

In 1998 Karla Faye Tucker became the first woman executed in Texas since the Civil War.

VIEWPOINT

1

The Death Penalty Is Unfairly Applied to Minorities

Christina Swarns

"Race and class remain critical factors in the decision of who lives and who dies."

In the following viewpoint, Christina Swarns argues that the justice system is racially biased against minority defendants, victims, and jurors. She states that black prisoners are more likely to be executed than white prisoners, and they are less likely to be given chances to overturn their death sentences. In addition to race being a factor of who gets executed, it is also a factor in who gets justice; the author argues that those who commit crimes against black victims are punished less severely than those who commit crimes against whites. Finally, she argues that blacks are often excluded from the juries of capital cases, which not only violates their civil rights, but also results in more black defendants being sentenced to death by all white juries. For these reasons, the author concludes that the capital punishment system is racist and must be abolished.

Christina Swarns is an attorney for the National Association for the Advancement of Colored People (NAACP).

AS YOU READ, CONSIDER THE FOLLOWING QUESTIONS:

1. What decision was made by the Supreme Court in 1976, and why?
2. According to the author, between 1995 and 2000, what was the ratio of black murderers to white murderers?
3. What was the content of a memo circulated to attorneys by a Texas prosecutor from 1963 to 1976?

I n 1972, the U.S. Supreme Court declared the death penalty unconstitutional. The Court found that because the capital-punishment
laws gave sentencers virtually unbridled discretion in deciding whether
or not to impose a death sentence, "The death sentence [was] dispro-
portionately carried out on the poor, the Negro, and the members of
unpopular groups."

In 1976, the Court reviewed the revised death-penalty statutes—which
are in place today—and concluded that they sufficiently restricted sen-
tencer discretion such that race and class would no longer play a pivotal
role in the life-or-death calculus. In
the 28 years since the reinstatement
of the death penalty, however, it has
become apparent that the Court was
wrong. Race and class remain critical factors in the decision of who
lives and who dies.

Fast Fact

Amnesty International USA
claims that blacks who murder whites are fifteen times
more likely to be executed
than if they murdered other
blacks.

A Lethal Handicap

Both race and poverty corrupt the
administration of the death penalty. Race severely disadvantages the
black jurors, black defendants, and black victims within the capital-
punishment system. Black defendants are more likely to be executed than white defendants. Those who commit crimes against black
victims are punished less severely than those who commit crimes
against white victims. And black potential jurors are often denied
the opportunity to serve on death-penalty juries. As far as the death

penalty is concerned, therefore, blackness is a proxy for worthlessness.

Poverty is a similar—and often additional—handicap. Because the lawyers provided to indigent defendants charged with capital crimes are so uniformly undertrained and undercompensated, the 90 percent of capitally charged defendants who lack the resources to retain a private attorney are virtually guaranteed a death sentence. Together, therefore, race and class function as an elephant on death's side of the sentencing scale.

Prosecutors Unfairly Target Blacks

When and how does race infect the death penalty system? . . .

Chief prosecutors, who are overwhelmingly white, make some of the most critical decisions vis-a-vis the death penalty. Because their decisions

Two activists demonstrate outside a Texas prison in protest of the large number of executions of low-income minorities.

In 2000 death penalty opponents march in New York to protest the huge number of minority executions in Texas under then-governor George W. Bush.

go unchecked, prosecutors have arguably the greatest unilateral influence over the administration of the death penalty.

Do prosecutors exercise their discretion along racial lines? Unquestionably yes. Prosecutors bring more defendants of color into the death-penalty system than they do white defendants. For example, a 2000 study by the U.S. Department of Justice reveals that between 1995 and 2000, 72 percent of the cases that the attorney general approved for death-penalty prosecution involved defendants of color. During that time, statistics show that there were relatively equal numbers of black and white homicide perpetrators.

Prosecutors also give more white defendants than black defendants the chance to avoid a death sentence. Specifically, prosecutors enter into plea bargains—deals that allow capitally charged defendants to receive a lesser sentence in exchange for an admission of guilt—with white defendants far more often than they do with defendants of color. Indeed, the Justice Department study found that white defendants were almost twice as likely as black defendants to enter into such plea agreements.

No Justice for Black Victims or Black Jurors

Further, prosecutors assess cases differently depending upon the race of the victim. Thus, the Department of Justice found that between 1995 and 2000, U.S. attorneys were almost twice as likely to seek the death

Critics of the death penalty in Los Angeles protest the pending execution of an African American man they claim was unfairly tried and sentenced to death in 2004.

A man demonstrates against the death penalty outside the Chesapeake courthouse where John Lee Malvo, an African American juvenile, is standing trial for murder.

penalty for black defendants accused of killing nonblack victims than for black defendants accused of killing black victims.

And, finally, prosecutors regularly exclude black potential jurors from service in capital cases. For example, a 2003 study of jury selection in Philadelphia capital cases, conducted by the Pennsylvania Supreme Court Commission on Race and Gender Bias in the Justice System, revealed that prosecutors used peremptory challenges—the power to exclude potential jurors for any reason aside from race or gender—to remove 51 percent of black potential jurors while excluding only 26 percent of nonblack potential jurors. Such bias has a long history: From 1963 to 1976, one Texas prosecutor's office instructed its lawyers to exclude all people of color from service on juries by distributing a memo containing the following language: "Do not take Jews, Negroes, Dagos [a derogatory name for Italians, Spaniards, or Portuguese], Mexicans or a member of any minority race on a jury, no matter how rich or how well educated." This extraordinary exercise of discretion harms black capital defendants because statistics reveal that juries containing few or no blacks are more likely to sentence black defendants to death.

Such blatant prosecutorial discretion has significantly contributed to the creation of a system that is visibly permeated with racial bias. Black defendants are sentenced to death and executed at disproportionate rates. For example, in Philadelphia, African American defendants are approximately four times more likely to be sentenced to death than similarly situated white defendants. And nationwide, crimes against white victims are punished more severely than crimes against black victims. Thus, although 46.7 percent of all homicide victims are black, only 13.9 percent of the victims of executed defendants are black. In some jurisdictions, all of the defendants on death row have white victims; in other jurisdictions, having a white victim exponentially increases a criminal defendant's likelihood of being sentenced to death. It is beyond dispute, therefore, that race remains a central factor in the administration of the death penalty.

EVALUATING THE AUTHORS' ARGUMENTS:

In the viewpoint you just read, the author argues that race is a critical factor in the death penalty system. In the following viewpoint, the author argues that one's actions are a critical factor in the death penalty system. After reading both viewpoints, which argument do you find more compelling? Why? Explain your reasoning.

The Death Penalty Is Fairly Applied to Minorities

Gregory Kane

In the following viewpoint, Gregory Kane contends that there is no evidence of racial bias in the administration of the death penalty. The author argues that the reason African Americans are executed more often than whites is because African Americans commit more crimes deserving of capital punishment. He uses the case of Napoleon Beazley, a black man on death row, to illustrate how, of his own free will, Beazley chose a life of crime over one of academic achievement. Kane urges the black community to stop finding excuses for why so many African Americans end up on death row and start dealing with the problems that put them there. The author urges African Americans to realize that Beazley, and other condemned prisoners like him, act of their own accord and are not on death row because of racism.

Gregory Kane is a regular columnist for the *Baltimore Sun*, from which this viewpoint was taken.

"Try as we might, black Americans can't blame whitey for this one."

I s there no African-American miscreant whose misdeeds are so vile
and contemptible that he cannot become a cause celebre in black
America?

Apparently not. The latest such candidate for the Victimhood
Sweepstakes African-Americans hold on an annual basis is Napoleon
Beazley, a 24-year-old black man on Texas' death row. In 1994, when he
was 17, Beazley shot John Luttig to death in an attempted carjacking.
There is little question about his guilt. 2 co-defendants testified against
him. Luttig was killed with a
handgun. Beazley was the only
one in his party of 3 thugs carrying one.

*Napoleon Beazley was executed in a Texas
prison for a murder he committed at the
age of seventeen.*

Undue Sympathy
for a Murderer

So what makes Beazley the object
of sympathy in the September
[2001] issue of *Savoy* magazine,
a periodical targeting a black audience? It's Beazley's age at the time
he so callously snuffed out Luttig's
life. He was "only" 17, a mere
juvenile, not responsible for his
actions. Or so the article, "Old
enough to die?" implies.

"At 17," the beginning of the
story by Shawn E. Rhea reads,
"Napoleon Beazley wasn't old
enough to buy cigarettes or vote,

but he was old enough to be sent to death row." This, dear reader, is what is passing for logic on the left [that is, liberal] side of the African-American political spectrum these days. Sophistry and specious argument rule the day. Because Beazley couldn't vote or buy a pack of Kools, the reasoning goes, he shouldn't be held accountable for cold-blooded murder.

Rhea then gives more details of Beazley's life. His victim gets an obligatory sentence or two, but the more we hear about Beazley, the less sympathy we have for him. He was not some misguided kid from an abusive background with irresponsible parents growing up in poverty. Rhea quotes one woman who said Beazley came from "a fine family with a good background." He starred in four sports in his Grapeland, Texas, high school. He was runner-up for Mr. Grapeland High, was voted Most Athletic in his senior year, served as president of his senior class and tutored some of his classmates. This guy, if he wanted to, could have been in college from the years 1995 to 1999.

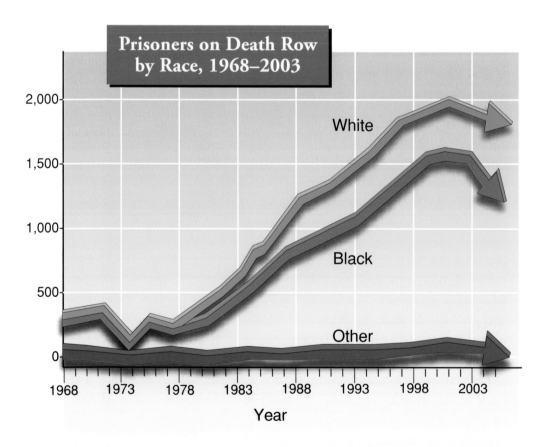

Source: *Capital Punishment 2003,* U.S. Department of Justice, Bureau of Justice Statistics, www.ojp.usdoj.gov.

An African American defendant refuses to rise as the jury enters the courtroom. Statistics show that more African Americans are convicted of capital crimes than Caucasians.

The Truth Hurts

But he didn't want to. Instead, he latched onto a gang of hoods and began selling drugs. Later, he got involved with Cedric and Donald Coleman, 2 brothers, and tried to carjack Luttig. The brothers testified against him and got 40 years apiece. Beazley got death and, now, fame as a victim of what is perceived as former Texas governor and now President George W. Bush's zeal for executing juveniles.

Let's take a reality check here. Bush didn't put Beazley on death row. Beazley did. Beazley guns down Luttig, and somehow Bush is the villain? That's the thinking among segments of black America. We black conservatives contend that most African-Americans reject this view. Those who don't, should. Because of guys like Beazley, white Americans view all of us as prone to criminality.

Why are there more black men in prison than in college? The black left whines, whimpers and asks that question almost daily. The truth, they say, hurts. In this case, it's downright excruciating, because the answer is: They choose to be there.

It's not because of white racism, or institutional racism, or poor education or poverty or even because that awful Uncle Tom, [Justice] Clarence Thomas, is on the Supreme Court. Beazley had a choice. He could have used his athletic ability and success as a student to get a college scholarship. Instead, he hung out with a bunch of rats and ended up on death row. Try as we might, black Americans can't blame whitey for this one.

We can blame ourselves. Who raises black boys into manhood? In 99 % of the cases, it's other black people. We instill the values, but there is a notion among our young men that crime is a cultural imperative. Why else would Beazley, with so much going for him and with a future bright as a sunrise on a cloudless horizon, choose to hang out with the criminal element?

Black America Must Not Make Excuses

He didn't reveal it in the *Savoy* article, but it shouldn't surprise us if Beazley fell into the trap of thinking that academic success was a "white" thing and that being a criminal was cool. There are some conservative critics of African-Americans who love to point to statistics that show blacks commit violent crimes far out of proportion to our numbers in the population. Few of these critics note that the problem is not new and is almost a century old.

In 1904, [the influential African-American writer] W.E.B. DuBois and other black scholars noted at the Ninth Atlanta Conference on Negro Crime that crime "is a dangerous and threatening phenomenon. It means

Whether the death penalty can ever be fairly applied to criminals regardless of race will continue to be a controversial legal issue.

large numbers of the freedmen's sons have not yet learned to be law-abiding citizens or steady workers, and until they do, the progress of the race, of the South, and of the Nation will be retarded."

By portraying Napoleon Beazley and others like him as victims, we make sure the "progress of the race" will remain impeded. Instead of holding Beazley and others accountable for their actions, we send them a message that no matter how heinous the crime they commit, black America will have their back.

Where is that damn DuBois now that we really need him?

EVALUATING THE AUTHORS' ARGUMENTS:

Christina Swarns is an attorney for the National Association for the Advancement of Colored People (NAACP), a liberal nonprofit organization that protects the rights of African Americans. Gregory Kane is an African American writer whose columns appear in conservative publications. Does knowing the authors' backgrounds influence your assessment of their arguments? Why or why not?

The Mentally Disabled Can Be Fairly Executed

Richard Lowry

"An adult, even with a low IQ, has more life experiences and maturity than a child."

In the following viewpoint, Richard Lowry uses the case of convicted murderer Daryl Atkins to argue that the mentally retarded are conscious of their crimes and should therefore be eligible to receive the death penalty. The author describes Atkins as a shrewd, calculating murderer who in killing his victim demonstrated his capacity for strategy and cognizance. Lowry contends that Atkins's lawyers misrepresented him as a barely functional simplistic person and in doing so abused the privilege exempting the profoundly retarded from being executed on the grounds that they do not know the difference between right and wrong. Furthermore, the author takes issue with the frequent claim that mentally retarded people are childlike, stating instead that they are mature adults who, regardless of their intelligence, have a life's worth of adult experiences to draw from. Lowry concludes that most mentally retarded offenders are culpable for their crimes and should therefore not be exempt from receiving the death penalty.

Richard Lowry is the editor of *National Review,* a conservative journal that features columns on various current events.

AS YOU READ, CONSIDER THE FOLLOWING QUESTIONS:
1. What is Daryl Atkins's reported IQ?
2. Why does the author cite Atkins's case as evidence that the justice system is working?
3. How does Lowry's account of Eric Nesbitt's murder contradict the contention that Atkins is not smart enough to understand the consequences of his actions?

In its decision [in June 2002] banning the execution of the mentally retarded, the Supreme Court made a poster boy of sorts of Daryl Atkins, the convicted murderer who challenged his death sentence on the grounds of his low IQ.

But Atkins, who supposedly has a 59 IQ and the mental capacity of a 9- to 12-year-old, really refutes the court's core contention—that executing the retarded is unconstitutionally "cruel and unusual" because low-IQ offenders can't be culpable for their crimes the way brighter people are.

The court reversed its own 1989 decision upholding such executions, mostly on the basis of opinion polls, which show that many people recoil from the idea of executing the retarded. They might not if they knew more about Daryl Atkins.

FAST FACT

A Gallup poll conducted in May 2002 found that 82 percent of Americans oppose the death penalty for the mentally retarded.

A Portrait of a Killer

On August 16, 1996, Atkins and his friend William Jones were hanging around Yorktown, Va., drinking and smoking dope, when they came up short on beer money.

The "mentally incompetent" Atkins asked a friend to borrow his handgun. He then went to a local convenience store with Jones and panhandled customers entering the store, including Eric Nesbitt, an airman from Langley Air Force Base.

When Nesbitt came out, the "barely functional" Atkins whistled at him as he was pulling away in his truck. Atkins pulled the gun on Nesbitt, jumped in the passenger side of the truck and ordered Nesbitt to let Jones drive.

The "simple-minded" Atkins took Nesbitt's wallet, removed $60, then noticed an ATM card. He told Jones to drive to the Crestar Bank and forced Nesbitt to remove $200. A security camera caught Atkins holding the gun on Nesbitt.

A surveillance photo shows Daryl Atkins, Eric Nesbitt (center), and William Jones shortly before Atkins killed Nesbitt. Atkins was spared the death penalty because of a mental disability.

Jones wanted to tie Nesbitt up and leave, but the "child-like" Atkins told Jones to drive to a secluded area. He then ordered Nesbitt out of the truck and shot him eight times.

At trial, the "clueless" Atkins maintained that Jones originally had the gun at the convenience store, then gave it to Atkins once he started driving (which supposedly accounted for the ATM photo), before finally taking the gun back in time to shoot Nesbitt.

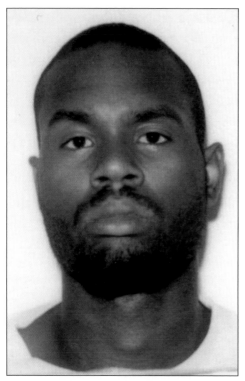

Daryl Atkins's case spurred the Supreme Court to rule that mentally retarded criminals cannot be executed.

Shrewd Enough to Play Dumb

Now, obviously the criminal-justice system cannot ignore mental retardation. And it doesn't—it is usually considered at a competency hearing, at trial and at sentencing.

The profoundly retarded are never executed. The tough calls are cases like that of Atkins, where the perpetrator is slow but functional, and perhaps shrewd enough to know the advantages of being dumb.

But these are exactly the sort of judgments of facts and culpability that juries are supposed to make.

In the Atkins case, a defense psychologist testified that based on an IQ test, Atkins was mildly retarded, but competent to stand trial and aware that it was wrong to kill someone. The prosecutor's psychologist, meanwhile, pointed out that Atkins knew who was president in 1961 and used complex words like "orchestra," "decimal" and "parable."

Rather than evidence of a "cruel and unusual" practice, therefore, the Atkins case is more an example of the justice system working in a perfectly reasonable manner.

The Mentally Retarded Are Culpable

Critics of capital punishment like to say a retarded criminal has "the mentality of a child." But this isn't so, because an adult, even with a low IQ, has more life experiences and maturity than a child.

Low-IQ people are, after all, people, their acts and motives highly individualistic and worthy of evaluation on a case-by-case basis.

"In light of the diverse capacities and life experiences of mentally retarded persons," a legal sage once wrote, "it cannot be said . . . that all mentally retarded people, by definition can never act with the level of culpability associated with the death penalty."

That sage was [Supreme Court justice] Sandra Day O'Connor in the 1989 Supreme Court decision upholding the execution of the retarded. [In 2002] she reversed herself, even though evidence for the soundness of her original decision was right in front of her—in the person of Daryl Atkins.

EVALUATING THE AUTHORS' ARGUMENTS:

In the viewpoints you just read, the author argues that regardless of their intelligence, mentally retarded people have significant life experience and thus should be held fully accountable for their crimes. In the following viewpoint, the author argues that retarded criminals have the mental capacity of a child and thus should not receive the harshest punishment for their crimes. In your opinion, whose argument is more convincing? Explain your reasoning.

The Mentally Disabled Cannot Be Fairly Executed

Jamie Fellner

"Mentally retarded persons simply do not qualify as among the most culpable offenders."

In the following viewpoint, Jamie Fellner contends that mentally retarded criminals should not be executed because they are uniquely disadvantaged in life and in court. It is widely accepted that the death penalty is supposed to be reserved for the worst offenders. Yet the author argues that because mentally retarded criminals often are incapable of understanding and controlling their actions, they do not constitute the most blameworthy of criminals. Furthermore, Fellner argues that because the mentally retarded have limited capacity for complex ideas, they often waive their access to important rights, or confess to crimes they did not commit. Prosecutors are likely to seek the death penalty against them because of a misplaced desire for victory, while jurors often mistake a mentally retarded criminal's carefree simplicity for remorselessness. The author concludes that while all executions

Jamie Fellner, "Beyond Reason: Executing Persons with Mental Retardation," *Human Rights,* Summer 2001.

violate human rights, it is especially wrong to impose the death penalty on mentally retarded criminals.

Jamie Fellner is an attorney with Human Rights Watch, a nonprofit organization that works to protect human rights around the world.

AS YOU READ, CONSIDER THE FOLLOWING QUESTIONS:
1. According to the author, what are three criteria used to determine if someone is mentally retarded?
2. Earl Washington Jr. was pardoned from prison in 2001. Why was he initially incarcerated?
3. According to Fellner, what are two ways in which mentally retarded people are disadvantaged during a trial?

A t least thirty-five men with mental retardation have been executed in the United States since 1976, when the death penalty was reinstated. No one knows exactly how many of the 3,700 people currently on death row have such a disability. Expert estimates range from 2 to 10 percent. Some of those sentenced to death have been so mentally impaired they did not fully understand their fate. Before his execution in 1985 for rape and murder, Morris Mason, with his intelligence quotient (IQ) of 62 to 66, asked for advice on what to wear to his funeral.

Starting as I do from the premise that all state-sponsored executions violate basic human rights, it is difficult to say any one execution is worse than another. Yet there is something so intrinsically senseless and cruel about executing people with limited mental development that many death penalty supporters are appalled by the practice. The death penalty is ostensibly limited to the most blameworthy persons. Mentally retarded people, however, are incapable of mature, calculated evil; in crucial ways their minds function like those of children. Their mental impairment not only limits their moral culpability, it also renders them uniquely vulnerable to miscarriages of justice. . . .

Mentally Retarded Criminals Are Less Culpable

Mental retardation is a lifelong condition of impaired mental development. According to the most widely used definition, it is characterized

Source: Sack. © 2001 by the *Star Tribune,* Minneapolis–St. Paul. Reproduced by permission.

by three criteria: subaverage intellectual functioning (an IQ score of approximately seventy or below), [1] limitations in the skills necessary for everyday life, and manifestation before the age of eighteen. . . .

Whatever the degree of retardation, all mentally retarded persons have a limited capacity for coping with life's challenges. They have grave difficulties with communication, learning, logic, strategic thinking, and planning. Their disability adversely affects their judgment, memory, and attention, as well as their capacity to understand abstract concepts. Their ability to exercise restraint and to weigh alternative courses of action is diminished. They have difficulty learning from experience and understanding cause-and-effect relationships.

Persons with mental retardation, including those who commit acts of deadly violence, may be incapable of fully controlling their actions, comprehending the consequences of their conduct, or understanding its moral implications. With a limited capacity for making genuine choices about how to act—a limitation that is exacerbated when they are

1. The average person's IQ in the United States is one hundred.

frightened, angry, or in stressful situations—mentally retarded persons simply do not qualify as among the most culpable offenders.

A Special Vulnerability

People with mental retardation are also uniquely and deeply vulnerable in criminal trials, a vulnerability that can be fatal when they are charged with capital crimes. They typically have difficulty comprehending abstract

In 1995 Herman Lee Hughes, a mentally retarded man, was convicted of murder and sentenced to death. His case is currently under appeal.

legal concepts, assisting in their own defense, or making informed choices regarding their rights. Eddie Mitchell, a retarded man on death row in Louisiana, waived his rights during his interrogation. When subsequently asked what "waiving his rights" meant, Mitchell raised his right hand and waved.

People with mental retardation are characteristically suggestible, eager to please persons in authority, and unable to cope with tension-filled situations. During police interrogations, most readily waive their right to remain silent and subsequently confess. Some even make false confessions, telling the police what they want to hear.

Earl Washington, Jr., a mentally retarded farmhand from rural Virginia with an IQ measured from fifty-seven to sixty-nine, confessed

Earl Washington Jr. (right) smiles at a news conference held after his release from prison in 2001. He was wrongfully convicted of murder.

during a lengthy police interrogation to a whole host of crimes, including the stabbing of a young woman in 1982. . . . The confession—which he subsequently recanted—largely consisted of Washington agreeing with what the police asked him and was laden with inaccuracies. For example, Washington told the police that the murder victim was black, even though she was white. He said he had kicked down her door, but it was undamaged. . . . DNA tests subsequently proved that someone else had committed the crime. After spending eighteen years behind bars, and coming at one point within nine days of being executed, Washington was pardoned last year and released from prison on February 12, 2001. . . .

Little Idea What Is Happening

Even when a defense lawyer presents evidence of the client's retardation, prosecutors are all too often more concerned with the professional or political ramifications of obtaining a "victory"—a death sentence—than with giving serious consideration to the ways mental retardation has affected the defendant's comprehension and conduct. Faced with pressure from the community and the victim's family, they do not want to "excuse" the crime or let an offender "off too easy." During trials they vigorously challenge the existence of mental retardation, minimize its significance, and suggest that although a capital defendant may "technically" be considered retarded, he nonetheless has "street smarts"—and hence should receive the highest penalty. . . .

Most tragically, when prosecutors insist on seeking the death penalty for mentally retarded offenders, jurors all too often comply. As James Ellis, a law professor and expert on mental retardation and the criminal justice system, has noted, "There's some kind of disconnect between people's moral understanding and the way the system of imposing the death penalty actually works." Faced with terrible crimes, jurors can fail to appreciate the difference between guilt and culpability and do not want to "condone" a murder. They see a defendant who is smiling, drawing pictures, or not acting "remorseful" in the courtroom, and they think it is because he or she is callous and heartless rather than understanding that a person with mental retardation may have little idea what is happening. . . .

It Is Wrong to Execute the Mentally Retarded

A growing public revulsion against executing persons with mental retardation is reflected in opinion surveys and political initiatives. Polls consistently show a preponderance of American people believe it is wrong to impose the ultimate state-sanctioned punishment on the mentally retarded. Even death penalty supporters oppose such executions. . . .

The greater the number of states that prohibit the execution of persons with mental retardation, the more likely the Court will conclude such executions run counter to the nation's evolving "standards of decency." Until then, the United States remains, to my knowledge, the only democracy whose jurisprudence expressly permits the execution of mentally retarded defendants and in which such executions are carried out.

EVALUATING THE AUTHORS' ARGUMENTS:

Authors Jamie Fellner and Richard Lowry disagree on whether it is fair to execute mentally retarded criminals. Fellner is an attorney for Human Rights Watch, an international human rights organization, while Lowry is the editor of a conservative weekly journal. Does knowing these authors' backgrounds influence your assessment of their arguments? Why or why not?

Innocent People Are Likely to Be Executed

George Ryan

"Our capital system is haunted by the demon of error."

In the following viewpoint, former governor George Ryan argues that because the death penalty is prone to error, those sentenced to death should have their death sentences reduced. He cites several cases in which innocent people were put on death row and also suggests the system unfairly sentences guilty people to die. He regrets that the capital punishment system that he once enthusiastically supported could be so prone to mistakes and lapses in fairness. Because lawmakers have refused to either reform or repeal the system, Ryan concludes that in the pursuit of justice and fairness all death sentences in the state of Illinois must be exchanged for lesser sentences.

George Ryan was the governor of Illinois from 1999 to 2003.

AS YOU READ, CONSIDER THE FOLLOWING QUESTIONS:
1. Why does the author express relief that the Illinois justice system can take twenty years to execute someone on death row?
2. How has Ryan's position on the death penalty changed since 1977?
3. What does the author refer to as "a catastrophic failure"?

George Ryan, speech at Northwestern University College of Law, Chicago, IL, January 11, 2003.

Four years ago [in 1999] I was sworn in as the 39th Governor of Illinois. That was just four short years ago; that's when I was a firm believer in the American System of Justice and the death penalty. I believed that the ultimate penalty for the taking of a life was administrated in a just and fair manner.

Today, 3 days before I end my term as Governor, I stand before you to explain my frustrations and deep concerns about both the administration and the penalty of death. . . .

Many Innocents Sit on Death Row

I never intended to be an activist on this issue. I watched in surprise as freed death row inmate Anthony Porter was released from jail. A free man, he ran into the arms of Northwestern University Professor Dave Protess who poured his heart and soul into proving Porter's innocence with his journalism students.

He was 48 hours away from being wheeled into the execution chamber where the state would kill him.

It would all be so antiseptic and most of us would not have even paused, except that Anthony Porter was innocent of the double murder for which he had been condemned to die.

Source: Catrow. © 2000 by Copley News Service. Reproduced by permission.

After Mr. Porter's case there was the report by *Chicago Tribune* reporters Steve Mills and Ken Armstrong documenting the systemic failures of our capital punishment system. Half of the nearly 300 capital cases in Illinois had been reversed for a new trial or resentencing.

Nearly Half!

33 of the death row inmates were represented at trial by an attorney who had later been disbarred or at some point suspended from practicing law.

Of the more than 160 death row inmates, 35 were African American defendants who had been convicted or condemned to die by all-white juries.

More than two-thirds of the inmates on death row were African American.

46 inmates were convicted on the basis of testimony from jailhouse informants.

I can recall looking at these cases and the information from the Mills/Armstrong series and asking my staff: How does that happen? How in God's name does that happen? I'm not a lawyer, so somebody explain it to me.

But no one could. Not to this day.

An Absolute Embarrassment

Then over the next few months, there were three more exonerated men, freed because their sentence hinged on a jailhouse informant or new DNA technology proved beyond a shadow of doubt their innocence.

We then had the dubious distinction of exonerating more men than we had executed. 13 men found innocent, 12 executed.

As I reported yesterday, there is not a doubt in my mind that the number of innocent men freed from our Death Row stands at 17, with the pardons of Aaron Patterson, Madison Hobley, Stanley Howard and Leroy Orange.

That is an absolute embarrassment. 17 exonerated death row inmates is nothing short of a catastrophic failure. But the 13, now 17 men, is just the beginning of our sad arithmetic in prosecuting murder cases. During the time we have had capital punishment in Illinois, there were at least 33 other people wrongly convicted on murder charges and exonerated. Since we reinstated the death penalty there are also 93 people—93—where our criminal justice system imposed the most severe sanction and later rescinded the sentence or even released them from custody because they were innocent.

How many more cases of wrongful conviction have to occur before we can all agree that the system is broken? . . .

The system of death in Illinois is so unsure that it is not unusual for cases to take 20 years before they are resolved. And thank God. If it had moved any faster, then Anthony Porter, the Ford Heights Four, Ronald Jones, Madison Hobley and the other innocent men we've exonerated might be dead and buried. . . .

A Seriously Flawed System

So when will the system be fixed? How much more risk can we afford? Will we actually have to execute an innocent person before the tragedy that is our capital punishment system in Illinois is really understood? This summer, a United States District court judge held the federal death penalty was unconstitutional and noted that with the number of recent exonerations based on DNA and new scientific technology we undoubtedly executed innocent people before this technology emerged.

As I prepare to leave office, I had to ask myself whether I could really live with the prospect of knowing that I had the opportunity to act, but that I failed to do so because I might be criticized. Could I take the chance that our capital punishment system might be reformed, that wrongful convictions might not occur, that enterprising journalism students might free more men from death row?[1] A system that's so fragile that it depends on young journalism students is seriously flawed.

In 1977, the Illinois legislature was faced with the momentous decision of whether to reinstate the death penalty in Illinois. I was a member of the General Assembly at that time and when I pushed the

1. The author is referring to the efforts of students at Northwestern University that resulted in the exoneration of a prisoner on death row.

Protesters outside a Texas prison oppose the death penalty on the grounds that people might face execution for crimes they did not commit.

green button in favor of reinstating the death penalty in this great State, I did so with the belief that whatever problems had plagued the capital punishment system in the past were now being cured. I am sure that most of my colleagues who voted with me that day shared that view.

But 20 years later, after affirming hundreds of death penalty decisions, [former Supreme Court] Justice [Harry] Blackmun came to the realization, in the twilight of his distinguished career that the death penalty remains fraught with arbitrariness, discrimination, caprice and mistake." He expressed frustration with a 20-year struggle to develop procedural and substantive safeguards. In a now famous dissent he wrote in 1994,

Legal safeguards to prevent the executions of innocent people have often failed, death penalty opponents like this woman in Florida claim.

Flaws in the judicial system moved former Illinois governor George Ryan to commute the sentences of all condemned prisoners before he left office in 2003.

"From this day forward, I no longer shall tinker with the machinery of death.". . .

I Must Act

I cannot say it more eloquently than Justice Blackmun.

The legislature couldn't reform it.

Lawmakers won't repeal it.

But I will not stand for it.

I must act.

Our capital system is haunted by the demon of error, error in determining guilt, and error in determining who among the guilty deserves to die. Because of all of these reasons today I am commuting the sentences of all death row inmates.

This is a blanket commutation. I realize it will draw ridicule, scorn and anger from many who oppose this decision. They will say I am usurping the decisions of judges and juries and state legislators. But as I have said, the people of our state have vested in me to act in the interest of justice. Even if the exercise of my power becomes my burden I will bear it. Our constitution compels it. I sought this office, and even in my final days of holding it I cannot shrink from the obligations to justice and fairness that it demands.

EVALUATING THE AUTHOR'S ARGUMENTS:

As governor of a state, George Ryan was personally responsible for overseeing the death penalty system and for excusing people from or condemning them to death. How do you think this unique position may have influenced the way he approached the issue? Do you think it enabled him to think clearer about the death penalty than other people, or do you think it clouded his vision on the matter? Or do you think it had no effect? Explain your answer.

Innocent People Are Not Likely to Be Executed

Ramesh Ponnuru

In the following viewpoint, Ramesh Ponnuru argues that wrongful executions are unlikely to take place under the death penalty because it is a highly accurate process with a 99.55 percent success rate. The majority of the people who death penalty opponents claim to be innocent are in fact guilty, according to the author, because opponents' definition of "innocent" makes no distinction between prisoners who were freed on a legal technicality and those who actually did not commit the crime. Ponnuru charges that death penalty opponents are misled by inflated numbers and concludes the capital punishment system is a highly reliable system in which innocent people are unlikely to be put to death.

Ramesh Ponnuru is a senior editor of the *National Review,* the journal from which this viewpoint was taken. His articles have also appeared in many newspapers, including the *New York Times,* the *Washington Post,* the *Wall Street Journal,* the *Financial Times, Newsday,* and the *New York Post.*

> *"Many of the 'innocents' . . . are probably guilty."*

Ramesh Ponnuru, "Bad List: A Suspect Roll of Death Row Innocents," *National Review,* vol. 54, September 16, 2002, pp. 27–28. Copyright © 2002 by National Review, Inc., 215 Lexington Ave., New York, NY 10016. Reproduced by permission.

A terrible injustice was done to Ray Krone. In 1992, he was sentenced to death for the murder of Kim Ancona, a Phoenix [Arizona] cocktail waitress. He spent three years on Death Row before his first conviction was overturned. On retrial, he was sentenced to life in prison. All the while, he maintained that he was innocent. Eventually, DNA analysis proved that he was telling the truth: Another man had committed the crime. In April of [2002], Krone was freed.

In Washington, D.C., Senator Russ Feingold [of Wisconsin] marked the occasion. "Krone," the Wisconsin Democrat said, was "the hundredth person to be released from Death Row in the modern death-penalty era"—since, that is, the Supreme Court allowed the practice to resume in 1976. "How many innocent Americans today sit in their prison cells wrongly accused, counting down the days until there are no more?" Feingold asked. "There have now been 100 exonerations and 766 executions since the early 1970s. In other words, for every seven to eight Death Row inmates executed by the states or federal government, one has been found innocent and released from Death Row. . . . One risk, one error, one mistake, is one too many. But 100 mistakes, proven mistakes, qualifies as a crisis. And a crisis calls for action." Feingold wants a national moratorium on the death penalty.

FAST FACT

When inmates are sentenced to death, they usually sit for an average of 10 years on death row while their case is repeatedly appealed. During this time, new evidence may come forth in a case, to which DNA testing can be applied. Most pro–death penalty sources claim that this exhaustive process prevents anyone who is innocent from actually being executed.

Failing that, he favors his colleague [Vermont senator] Patrick Leahy's Innocence Protection Act, which backers say would improve the administration of the death penalty.

Technically Innocent, but Still Guilty

Krone's case is certainly disturbing. But have there really been 100 such "proven mistakes," as Feingold put it, in the last quarter century? The senator, like the many others who make this claim, relies on the "Innocence List" compiled by the Death Penalty Information Center [DPIC], a group that opposes capital punishment. According to its list, the total number of people who spent time on Death Row but were later exonerated is now up to 102.

But most of the cases on the list are very different from that of Ray Krone. Nobody is going to make a TV movie anytime soon about Jonathan Treadaway, another of DPIC's "Cases of Innocence." Treadaway was convicted in 1975 for sodomizing and murdering a six-year-old boy.

After spending ten years in prison for a murder he did not commit, Ray Krone (in cap) was cleared by DNA evidence that emerged in 2002.

His palm prints were found outside the victim's bedroom window, and he said that he could not explain their presence. Pubic hairs on the victim's body were similar to his.

But the Arizona supreme court reversed his conviction. The trial court had admitted evidence that Treadaway had committed sexual acts with a 13-year-old boy three years before the murder. The court held that to be irrelevant without "expert medical testimony" that this act demonstrated a continuing propensity to commit such acts. The court also ordered that at Treadaway's retrial, his statements about the palm prints not be admitted. Treadaway had made those statements voluntarily, but without being advised of his Miranda rights[1] or waiving those rights. Finally, the court excluded some evidence that three months before the murder, Treadaway had been found naked in a young boy's bedroom trying to strangle the boy.

Treadaway didn't get off Death Row because it was proven that the cops had the wrong man. Technicalities spared him.

No Exoneration

Jeremy Sheets, another of DPIC's "innocents," got off Death Row because the key witness against him couldn't testify. That was his best friend, Adam Barnett, who told the police that the two of them—both white men—had been angry about all the white women they knew who were dating black men. To get even, they kidnapped and raped a black high-school student. Barnett said that Sheets had then stabbed her to death. Barnett committed suicide in jail. Sheets was sentenced to death on the basis of Barnett's taped confession (and Sheets's own testimony, which the jury found unbelievable). The Nebraska supreme court reversed his conviction because Sheets's lawyer had not been able to cross-examine the dead Barnett. Sheets walked.

The lead police investigator in the case called the result a "travesty," but it was probably the right legal call. What it wasn't was an "exoneration" of Sheets.

John Henry Knapp confessed to the arson-murder of his children and then recanted the confession. He was tried three times. Twice juries hung 7-5 for conviction; in between, he was found guilty and sentenced to

---

1. Miranda rights are warnings given by police to criminal suspects advising them of their right to have a lawyer present for interrogations and their right to remain silent.

Death row inmate Jeremy Sheets (right) was spared execution for a 1992 murder as the result of a legal technicality.

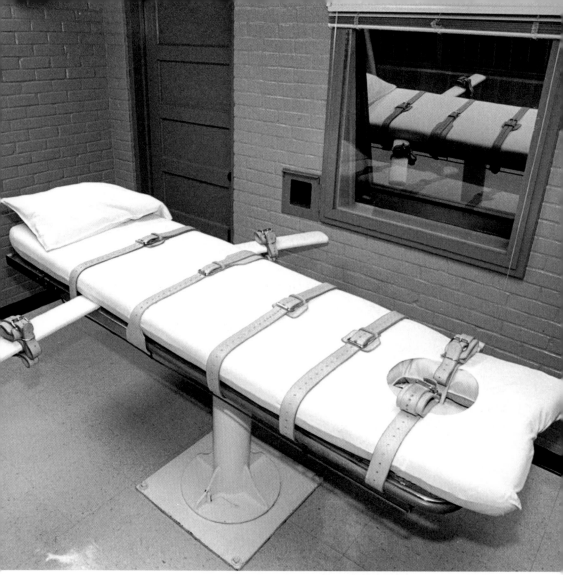

Statistics show that innocent people are unlikely to face the death penalty. In fact, of the 7,000 inmates on Death Row in modern times, only 32 were exonerated by DNA and other evidence.

death. Eventually the case was settled with a plea bargain. He's on the "Innocence List," too.

32 Out of 7,000—a 99.55 Percent Success Rate

In twelve of the cases on DPIC's list, DNA evidence indicates that the men on Death Row should never have been put there. In another 20 or so, there is other evidence to the same effect. In around 32 cases, then, it has been proven that men on Death Row were innocent of the crime charged. (That's out of more than 7,000 people on Death Row in the modern era.)

No such thing has been proved in the other cases. In some of them, the details are sketchy. Some death sentences were reversed in unpublished opinions. Some cases had to be abandoned because evidence deteriorated with the passage of time. In other cases, people who had participated in murders were removed from Death Row because it was not known whether they had actually pulled the trigger or struck the fatal blow themselves. They were hardly "innocent." There are at least as many Treadaways as Krones on the list. All of them are treated by DPIC, equivalently, as "innocent" and "exonerated."

Richard Dieter, executive director of DPIC, says that former Death Row inmates deserve a presumption of innocence when the charges against them are dismissed. They are indeed entitled to a legal presumption of innocence (in general: John Henry Knapp isn't). But the list leads people to think that innocence has been proven when the most that can be said is that the legal system cannot establish guilt beyond a reasonable doubt. Most of the people who refer to the list clearly have no idea that many of the "innocents" on it are probably guilty.

EVALUATING THE AUTHORS' ARGUMENTS:

In the viewpoint you just read, the author argues that it is very rare that an innocent person will be put on death row. In the previous viewpoint, the author makes the point that even one innocent person condemned to death is too many. In your opinion, must the death penalty be 100 percent foolproof in order for it to be acceptable? Why or why not? Explain your reasoning.

FACTS ABOUT THE DEATH PENALTY

The Death Penalty Around the World
According to Amnesty International:

- The United States is among seventy-eight countries that use the death penalty as punishment for crime.
- In 2003, 84 percent of all known executions occurred in China, Iran, Vietnam, and the United States.
- Since 1990, the countries that have executed juvenile offenders include China, the Democratic Republic of Congo, Iran, Nigeria, Pakistan, Saudi Arabia, the United States, and Yemen. Of these, the United States has carried out the most executions of juvenile offenders, nineteen since 1990.
- Of the countries that allow the death penalty, five use lethal injection (the most common form of execution in the United States). Seventy-five countries use firing squads, fifty-nine use hanging, six use stoning, and three use beheading (Congo, Saudi Arabia, and United Arab Emirates).
- Canada, Australia, and most of Europe have abolished the death penalty for all crimes.
- The United States, much of South America, and Asia have retained the death penalty for certain crimes.

The Death Penalty in the United States

- Since 1930, 4,775 people have been executed in the United States.
- A federal moratorium was imposed on the death penalty from 1967 to 1976, during which time no one was executed.
- The death penalty is allowable under federal military and civilian law.
- Thirty-eight states have retained the death penalty.
- The twelve states that have abolished the death penalty are Alaska, Hawaii, Iowa, Maine, Massachusetts, Michigan, Minnesota, North Dakota, Rhode Island, Vermont, West Virginia, and Wisconsin.
- In 1846, Michigan became the first state to abolish the death penalty. Rhode Island abolished it in 1852, followed by Wisconsin in 1853.

- In the thirty-eight states that enact the death penalty, five different methods of execution are legal: lethal injection, electrocution, lethal gas, firing squad, and hanging. Lethal injection is the most common form of execution.
- In some states, the method of execution depends on when the crime was committed. For example, in Georgia, inmates may be executed by electrocution if they committed their crime prior to May 1, 2000. If they committed their crime after this date, they will die by lethal injection.
- In some states, such as Arizona or California, inmates may elect whether they are executed by lethal injection or lethal gas. In Arizona, an inmate may have the option of choosing between electrocution and lethal injection.
- Over two thousand of America's death row inmates have been awaiting execution for more than six years.
- The United States has executed ten women since 1976. As of 2002 there were fifty-one women on death row.
- Each state has different rules regarding who can witness an execution. In Oregon, the immediate family of the victim, including parents, spouse, siblings, children, and grandparents, can watch an execution. In North Carolina, witnesses are limited to two people from the victim's family. In Georgia, no witnesses are allowed.
- Out of the states that permit the death penalty, Texas uses the death penalty the most. It has executed 336 people since 1977. Virginia is next with 94 executions; then Oklahoma, with 75, Missouri, 61, and Florida, which has executed 59 people since 1977.
- Of the states that permit the death penalty, Colorado, Idaho, New Mexico, Tennessee, and Wyoming are the states that use the death penalty least often. Since 1977 they have each put one person to death.
- According to the Death Penalty Information Center, since 1982 thirty-six executions have had complications, including people catching on fire, experiencing violent spasms, heavy bleeding from the face, choking, or other complications that resulted in a prolonged death.

According to the National Center for Policy Analysis:

- The death penalty is invoked in fewer than one in every five hundred homicide cases nationwide.

- Every execution results in approximately eighteen fewer murders.
- Since 1900, it has not been proven that any innocent people have been put to death in the United States.

According to the National Coalition to Abolish the Death Penalty:

- A single death penalty case, from the point of arrest to execution, ranges from $1 million to $3 million per case. Other studies have estimated the cost to be as high as $7 million. In contrast, cases resulting in life imprisonment average around $500,000 each, including cost of incarceration.

The Death Penalty and Race

According to the National Coalition to Abolish the Death Penalty:

- The odds of receiving a death sentence in Philadelphia are 38 percent higher when the defendant is black.
- Since 1977, blacks and whites have been the victims of murders in almost equal numbers, yet 80 percent of the people executed in that period were convicted of murders involving white victims.

According to Amnesty International:

- African Americans account for 42 percent of current death row inmates, yet make up 12 percent of the population.

According to Pro Death Penalty.com:

- Whites are twice as likely to be executed for committing murder as are their black counterparts.
- Whites sentenced to death are executed seventeen months more quickly than blacks.

National Surveys About the Death Penalty

According to a Gallup poll taken in May 2004:

- 62 percent of those surveyed did not believe the death penalty was a deterrent to committing murder, yet 71 percent supported executing a person convicted of homicide.
- 50 percent of those surveyed thought the death penalty was a better punishment for murder over life in prison; 46 percent said they thought life in prison was a more appropriate penalty for murder.
- 23 percent of those surveyed said the death penalty was imposed too often, 25 percent said it was imposed appropriately, and 48 percent said the death penalty was not imposed often enough.

- 55 percent of those surveyed said they believed the death penalty was applied fairly, while 39 percent said they believed it was applied unfairly.

In a May 2003 Gallup poll:

- 73 percent of those surveyed believed that an innocent person had probably been wrongly executed.

In a May 2002 Gallup poll:

- 69 percent of people surveyed opposed applying the death penalty to juvenile offenders.
- 75 percent opposed applying the death penalty to the mentally ill, while 82 percent opposed sentencing the mentally retarded to death.

ORGANIZATIONS TO CONTACT

The editors have compiled the following list of organizations concerned with the issues debated in this book. The descriptions are derived from materials provided by the organizations. All have publications or information available for interested readers. The list was compiled on the date of publication of the present volume; the information provided here may change. Be aware that many organizations take several weeks or longer to respond to inquiries, so allow as much time as possible.

Amnesty International USA (AI)
322 Eighth Ave., New York, NY 10001
(212) 807-8400
fax: (212) 627-1451
Web site: www.amnesty-usa.org

Amnesty International is an independent worldwide movement working impartially for the release of all prisoners of conscience, fair, and prompt trials for political prisoners, and an end to torture and executions. AI is funded by donations from its members and supporters throughout the world. AI has published several books and reports, including *Fatal Flaws: Innocence and the Death Penalty.*

Canadian Coalition Against the Death Penalty (CCADP)
PO Box 38104, 550 Eglinton Ave. West
Toronto, ON M5N 3A8 Canada
(416) 693-9112
fax: (416) 686-1630
e-mail: ccadp@home.com
Web site: www.ccadp.org

CCADP is a not-for-profit international human rights organization dedicated to educating on alternatives to the death penalty worldwide and to providing emotional and practical support to death row inmates, their families, and the families of murder victims. The center releases pamphlets and periodic press releases, and its Web site includes a student resource center providing research information on capital punishment.

Capital Punishment Project, American Civil Liberties Union (ACLU)
125 Broad St., 18th Fl., New York, NY 10004
(212) 549-2500
fax: (212) 549-2646
Web site: www.aclu.org

The project is dedicated to abolishing the death penalty. The ACLU believes that capital punishment violates the Constitution's ban on cruel and unusual punishment as well as the requirements of due process and equal protection under the law. It publishes and distributes numerous books and pamphlets, including *The Case Against the Death Penalty* and *Frequently Asked Questions Concerning the Writ of Habeas Corpus and the Death Penalty.*

Death Penalty Focus of California
870 Market St., Suite 859, San Francisco, CA 94102
(415) 243-0143
fax: (415) 243-0994
e-mail: info@deathpenalty.org
Web site: www.deathpenalty.org

Death Penalty Focus of California is a nonprofit organization dedicated to the abolition of capital punishment through grassroots organization, research, and the dissemination of information about the death penalty and its alternatives. It publishes the quarterly newsletter *The Sentry.*

Death Penalty Information Center (DPIC)
1320 Eighteenth St. NW, 2nd Fl., Washington, DC 20036
(202) 293-6970
fax: (202) 822-4787
e-mail: pbernstein@deathpenaltyinfo.org
Web site: www.deathpenaltyinfo.org

DPIC conducts research into public opinion on the death penalty. The center believes capital punishment is discriminatory and excessively costly and that it may result in the execution of innocent persons. It publishes numerous reports, such as *Millions Misspent: What Politicians Don't Say About the High Costs of the Death Penalty, Innocence and the Death Penalty: Assessing the Danger of Mistaken Executions,* and *With Justice for Few: The Growing Crisis in Death Penalty Representation.*

Justice Fellowship (JF)
PO Box 16069, Washington, DC 20041-6069
(703) 904-7312
fax: (703) 478-9679
Web site: www.justicefellowship.org

This Christian organization bases its work for reform of the justice system on the concept of victim-offender reconciliation. It does not take a position on the death penalty, but it publishes the pamphlet *Capital Punishment: A Call to Dialogue.*

Justice for All (JFA)
PO Box 55159, Houston, TX 77255
(713) 935-9300
fax: (713) 935-9301
e-mail: info@jfa.net
Web site: www.jfa.net

Justice for All is a not-for-profit criminal justice reform organization that supports the death penalty. Its activities include circulating online petitions to keep violent offenders from being paroled early, and publishing the monthly newsletter *The Voice of Justice.*

Lamp of Hope Project
PO Box 305, League City, Texas 77574-0305
e-mail: aspanhel@airmail.net
Web site: www.lampofhope.org

The project was established and is run primarily by Texas death row inmates. It works for victim-offender reconciliation and for the protection of the civil rights of prisoners, particularly the right of habeas corpus appeal. It publishes and distributes the periodic *Texas Death Row Journal.*

Lincoln Institute for Research and Education
1001 Connecticut Ave. NW, Suite 1135, Washington, DC 20036
(202) 223-5112

The institute is a conservative think tank that studies public policy issues affecting the lives of black Americans, including the issue of the death penalty, which it favors. It publishes the quarterly *Lincoln Review.*

National Coalition to Abolish the Death Penalty (NCADP)
1436 U St. NW, Suite 104, Washington, DC 20009
(202) 387-3890
fax: (202) 387-5590
e-mail: info@ncadp
Web site: www.ncadp.org

The National Coalition to Abolish the Death Penalty is a collection of more than 115 groups working together to stop executions in the United States. The organization compiles statistics on the death penalty. To further its goal, the coalition publishes *Legislative Action to Abolish the Death Penalty,* information packets, pamphlets, and research materials.

National Criminal Justice Reference Service (NCJRS)
U.S. Department of Justice, PO Box 6000, Rockville, MD 20849-6000
(301) 519-5500
toll free: (800) 851-3420
e-mail: askncjrs@ncjrs.org
Web site: www.ncjrs.org

The National Criminal Justice Reference Service is one of the most extensive sources of information on criminal and juvenile justice in the world. For a nominal fee, this clearinghouse provides topical searches and reading lists on many areas of criminal justice, including the death penalty. It publishes an annual report on capital punishment.

FOR FURTHER READING

Books

Mumia Abu-Jamal, *All Things Censored.* New York: Seven Stories Press, 2000. The life story of an inmate on death row.

Amnesty International, *On the Wrong Side of History: Children and the Death Penalty in the USA.* New York: Amnesty International USA, 1998. A publication by Amnesty International, a human rights organization that actively argues against the death penalty.

Jan Arriens, ed., *Welcome to Hell: Letters and Writings from Death Row.* Boston: Northeastern University Press, 1997. A collection of letters written by men and women on death row.

Stuart Banner, *The Death Penalty: An American History.* Boston: Harvard University Press, 2002. An overview of American attitudes toward capital punishment throughout history.

Hugo Adam Bedau et al., *Debating the Death Penalty: Should America Have Capital Punishment? The Experts on Both Sides Make Their Best Case.* New York: Oxford University Press, 2003. A collection of essays that explore the pros and cons of capital punishment.

Walter Berns, *For Capital Punishment.* Lanham, MD: University Press of America, 2000. The author thoroughly explores the penal system and criminal law and concludes that sentencing criminals to death is the best way to deliver justice.

Shirley Dicks, *Death Row: Interviews with Inmates, Their Families, and Opponents of Capital Punishment.* New York: iUniverse.com, 2001. This book, written by the mother of a man who was executed in Tennessee for a crime she claims he did not commit, explores how the poor are disadvantaged by the legal system.

John F. Galliher et al., *America Without the Death Penalty: States Leading the Way.* Boston: Northeastern University Press, 2002. The authors provide an in-depth study of the twelve states that have abolished the death penalty.

John Grabowski, *The Death Penalty.* San Diego: Lucent Books, 1999. Traces the history of the death penalty and explores varying opinions held on the subject. Excellent for young readers.

James S. Hirsch, *Hurricane: The Miraculous Journey of Rubin Carter.* Waterville, ME: Thorndike Press, 2000. The story of Rubin "Hurricane" Carter, a former boxer who spent twenty-two years in prison for a murder he did not commit.

Jesse Jackson, *Legal Lynching: Racism, Injustice, and the Death Penalty.* New York: Marlowe, 1996. Jesse Jackson, an American religious leader and public speaker, explores the ties between racism, innocence, and the death penalty in the American legal system.

Michael Mello, *Deathwork: Defending the Condemned.* Minneapolis: University of Minnesota Press, 2002. Written by a former capital public defender, this moving work offers a behind-the-scenes look at the life and work of a death row lawyer and his clients.

Louis P. Pojman and Jeffrey Reiman, *The Death Penalty: For and Against.* Lanham, MD: Rowman & Littlefield, 1998. The authors, social and political philosophers, each take opposing sides to illustrate key arguments in the debate over the death penalty.

Helen Prejean, *Dead Man Walking.* New York: Vintage Books, 1993. Written by a nun who provided spiritual guidance to a convicted killer on death row. A moving personal memoir and an intimate look at America's prison system.

Periodicals

George M. Anderson, "Don't Kill My Killer," *America,* March 1, 2004.

Emily Bazelon, "The Foolproof Death Penalty," *New York Times Magazine,* December 12, 2004.

Beverly Beckham, "Justice Can't Be Built on Executions Alone," *Boston Herald,* May 4, 2004.

Hugo Adam Bedau, "Causes and Consequences of Wrongful Conviction," *Current,* March/April 2003.

——, "Death's Dwindling Dominion: Public Opinion Is Shifting Against the Death Penalty. What Will It Take to Abolish It?" *American Prospect,* July 2004.

Thomas F. Bertonneau, "Pro: Execution Gives Justice to Forgotten Victim," *Detroit News,* June 3, 2001.

John D. Bessler, "America's Death Penalty: Just Another Form of Violence," *Phi Kappa Phi Forum,* Winter 2002.

Michael D. Bradbury, "The Death Penalty Is an Affirmation of the Sanctity of Life," *Los Angeles Times,* September 24, 2000.

Peter Bronson, "A Cruel Penalty for Victims," Enquirer.com, February 3, 2003.

Roger Clegg, "The Color of Death," *National Review,* June 11, 2001.

Richard Cohen, "The Vain Search for Deadly Accuracy," *Washington Post,* May 1, 2000.

Ann Coulter, "O.J. Was 'Proved Innocent,' Too," *Human Events,* June 20, 2000.

Denver Post, "Death Penalty Losing Its Grip," November 21, 2004.

Robert F. Drinan, "The World Has Judged Electrocution as Inhumane," *National Catholic Reporter,* January 14, 2000.

Thomas R. Eddlem, "Ten Anti-Death Penalty Fallacies," *New American,* June 3, 2002.

Don Feder, "It's Hard to Pardon the Excuses Given by Death Penalty Opponents," *Insight on the News,* vol. 17, 2001.

Thomas Flemming, "The Christian Militant," *Chronicles,* October 2003.

Brian Forst, "Taming the Justice Error Demon," *Responsive Community,* Fall 2003.

William Glaberson, "Nine Years Later, Death Penalty Is Still Murky," *New York Times,* April 25, 2004.

Grand Rapids Press, "Wrong Penalty for Murder; There Is No Going Back When a Person Is Put to Death," February 26, 2004.

H.D.S. Greenway, "McVeigh's Fate Isn't Humane," *Boston Globe,* May 16, 2001.

Steven W. Hawkins, "Do We Need the Death Penalty? It Is Immoral and Ineffective," *World & I,* September 2002.

Christopher Hitchens, "Tinkering with the Death Machine," *Nation,* July 22–29, 2002.

Jeff Jacoby, "Old Enough to Kill. Old Enough to Die?" *Boston Globe,* October 21, 2004.

Hank Kalet, "A Penalty for All of Us," *Progressive Populist,* vol. 7, 2001.

William J. Leahy, "Justice Isn't Served by Executions," *Boston Herald,* January 29, 2004.

Charles Levendosky, "Against Civilization: Executing Child Offenders," *Liberal Opinion Week,* January 17, 2000.

Todd Lindberg, "An Execution and Its Witnesses," *Weekly Standard,* May 14, 2001.

Adam Liptak, "On Death Row, a Battle over the Fatal Cocktail," *New York Times,* September 16, 2004.

Roger Mahony, "New Ethic: Justice Without Vengeance," *Origins,* June 8, 2000.

Eugene H. Methvin, "Death Penalty Is Fairer than Ever," *Wall Street Journal,* May 10, 2000.

Iain Murray, "More Executions, Fewer Deaths?" *American Outlook,* Fall 2001.

National Catholic Reporter, "Dissent and the Death Penalty," July 2, 2004.

Norm Pattis, "We Kill What's Good in Us When We Kill What's Bad," *Connecticut Law Tribune,* October 18, 2004.

Ramesh Ponnuru, "Not So Innocent," *National Review,* October 1, 2004.

Dennis Prager, "More Innocents Die When We Don't Have Capital Punishment," Townhall.com, June 17, 2003.

San Francisco Chronicle, "No Mercy for Scott Peterson," December 14, 2004.

Mark Sappenfield, "Growing Role of Emotion in Jury Verdicts; Peterson Case Shows How Jurors Can Make Decisions, Even About Death Penalty, Based on Personal Demeanor," *Christian Science Monitor,* December 15, 2004.

Sally Satel, "It's Crazy to Execute the Insane," *Wall Street Journal,* March 14, 2002.

Dudley Sharp, "Why Some 'Juvenile' Murderers Should Qualify for the Death Penalty," Dpinfo.com, 2004.

Michelangelo Signorile, "Killing the 20th Hijacker," *New York Press,* April 4, 2002.

Tom Teepen, "McVeigh Execution Will Bring More Death, Not Closure," *Cox Newspapers,* May 8, 2001.

Daniel E. Troy, "Our Innate Morality Demands Execution," *Los Angeles Times,* August 7, 2001.

Jay Varner, "Not a More Humane Way to Kill," *New Abolitionist,* December 2001.

Washington Times, "Teens, Murder, and the Supreme Court," October 23, 2002.

Web Sites

The Case Against the Death Penalty (http://users.rcn.com/mwood/deathpen.html). Brief articles on various aspects of capital punishment from an anti–death penalty perspective.

Clark County Prosecuting Attorney's Office—The Death Penalty (www.clarkprosecutor.org/html/death/death.htm). This exhaustive site includes a helpful time line of capital punishment in the United States, along with over a thousand links to both pro-and-con articles on the death penalty.

The Moratorium Campaign (www.moratoriumcampaign.org). This site contains many good links to a variety of anti–death penalty Web sites and activist programs.

Pro–Death Penalty.com (www.prodeathpenalty.com). This site has an extensive collection of pro–death penalty articles, along with helpful links and charts that analyze executions on a state-by-state basis. A section on public polls taken on the death penalty is especially interesting.

Wesley Lowe's Pro Death Penalty Page (www.wesleylowe.com/cp.html). Brief articles on various aspects of capital punishment from a pro–death penalty perspective.

You Can't Pardon a Corpse (www.compusmart.ab.ca/deadmantalking). This anti–death penalty Web site contains interesting articles and links to the writings of inmates on death row.

INDEX

ABA Journal, 20
African Americans
  are more likely to be executed
    than whites, 86–87
  are often excluded from
    juries, 90–91
  percent of murders in U.S.
    committed by, 96
  prosecutors are more likely to
    seek death penalty for,
    87–90
  whites vs., on death row, 94,
    113
American Medical Association
  (AMA), 37
Ancona, Kim, 120
Armstrong, Ken, 113
Atkins, Daryl, 99, 100–102
Autry, James, 37

Baltimore Sun (newspaper), 92
Barnett, Adam, 122
Beazley, Napoleon, 92, 93–94,
  96
Benjamin, Charles, 54
Blackmun, Harry, 116–17
Brennan, William, 69, 70
Brown, Nicolai, 78
Bufacchi, Vittorio, 32
Bush, George W., 75

Cabana, Don, 38

Chicago Tribune (newspaper),
  113
Clegg, Roger, 96
Clements, Diane, 14
Clinton, Bill, 28
Coleman, Cedric, 95
Coleman, Donald, 95
Constitution, U.S. *See* Eighth
  Amendment
Cooey, Richard, 79
Council of Europe, 12
Cushing, Renny, 26

Dayan, Marshall, 66
death penalty
  as act of justice, 15
  does not reduce crime, 67–71
    con, 62–63, 75–77
  increases violence in society,
    79–83
  is about revenge, 28
    con, 19
  is a just punishment for mur-
    der, 18–19, 43–44
  life is honored by, 21–22
  poverty corrupts administra-
    tion of, 86
  as violation of human rights,
    11–13
  see also execution(s)
Death Penalty Information
  Center, 67, 121

PICTURE CREDITS

Cover photo: AP/Wide World Photos

AP/Wide World Photos, 12, 19, 27, 34, 42 (inset), 45, 46, 49 (inset), 55, 61, 63, 64, 68, 70, 73, 81, 95, 101, 102, 107, 108, 115, 116, 117, 121, 123

Armando Arorizo/EPA/Landov, 89

Jim Bourg/Reuters/Landov, 22 (inset)

© Michael Brennan/CORBIS, 82

Paul Buck/EPA/Landov, 124

Paul S. Howell/Getty Images, 87

© Mark Jenkinson/CORBIS, 16

© Kevin Lamarque/Reuters/CORBIS, 56

Brendan McDermid/Reuters/Landov, 49

Jeff Mitchell/Reuters/Landov, 29

Jason Reed/Reuters/Landov, 90

© Reuters/CORBIS, 13, 14, 42, 75

Reuters/Landov, 22, 50, 84, 93

© Royalty-Free/CORBIS, 97

Sue Santillan, 38, 69, 76, 94

© Touhig Sion/CORBIS SYGMA, 88

© F. Carter Smith/CORBIS SYGMA, 36

© Greg Smith/CORBIS, 59

Emile Wamsteker/Bloomberg News/Landov, 23

Betty Wells/Getty Images, 52

ABOUT THE EDITOR

Lauri S. Friedman earned her bachelor's degree in religion and political science from Vassar College. Much of her studies there focused on political Islam, and she produced a thesis on the Islamic Revolution in Iran titled *Neither West, Nor East, But Islam*. She also holds a preparatory degree in flute performance from the Manhattan School of Music, and is pursuing a master's degree in history at San Diego State University. She has edited over ten books for Greenhaven Press, including *At Issue: What Motivates Suicide Bombers?*, *At Issue: How Should the United States Treat Prisoners in the War on Terror?*, and *Introducing Issues with Opposing Viewpoints: Terrorism*. She currently lives near the beach in San Diego with her yellow lab, Trucker.